THINK IT OVER

with
Father Gordon Albion

THE ⬡ UNIVERSE

for Anne Birrell

Books by the same author:

Charles I and the Court of Rome
The Story of the Church
The Church in the Modern World (with Robert Nowell)
Think It Over with Father Gordon Albion (1974)
Because You Belong to Christ
Christians Awake

First published in Great Britain in 1979
by The Universe
Associated Catholic Publications Ltd
33-39 Bowling Green Lane
London EC1R 0AB

ISBN 0 904359 23 9

Printed and bound in Great Britain
by Billing & Sons Ltd
of Guildford, Surrey.
Photoset by News Photosetting Services Ltd
Skelmersdale, Lancashire.

CONTENTS

The Church's Year:

FOREWORD

Canon Gordon Albion's first-class mini-sermons have been playing to an audience of half a million or more every week in *The Universe* almost without interruption for more than 40 years — easily outstripping *The Mousetrap*.

I and my predecessors as Editor during that time have received a steady stream of enthusiastic letters from the readers, who clearly gain great inspiration and comfort from what Canon Albion writes. A lady has recently written to me to say that she has been cutting out the *Thought for the Week* articles for many years and pasting them in a scrap book for her three grandchildren.

I am only too delighted that these little gems of inspiration are now appearing in book form so that a permanent record will be available not only for our grandchildren but for their grandchildren in turn.

Christopher Monckton

The Hon. Christopher Monckton
Editor, *The Universe*

PREFACE

I made my first contribution to *The Universe* over forty years ago, in 1936. It was an editorial on Anglican Orders! This was followed by the occasional piece, usually on an historical subject. It was not until November 1956 that I began a regular weekly column. Called *Talking Point,* it invited critical comments, during and after the Second Vatican Council. Later, in 1971, I was asked to submit a shorter, reflective feature, which became the present *Thought for the Week.*

The popularity of this prompted the publication of one hundred of the articles. The book was soon out of print. This "second collection" is kindly being published by *The Universe* in response to frequent requests. I am grateful to Canon Paul Taylor of Cambridge for choosing and arranging the articles. I hope that this selection will please you.

Gordon Albion

GOD AND CHRIST MATTER

The besetting sin of our day is apathy towards Divine Truth and indifference to Christ who came to teach it. At a conservative estimate, 75 per cent of our fellow countrymen are quite content to live out their lives as if God and religion don't matter. They find a good deal of hypocrisy and cant among Church people and so write religion off as a bad bet. They'd rather not be bothered — thanks very much.

Now that's just where they're wrong. You can and you must be bothered if you think at all. God isn't the monopoly of the churchgoer and the Bible puncher.

On Sunday mornings, down in the country, you often see club cyclists pumping away for dear life at their pedals, noses well down over the handlebars. Now, if you saw one of these energetic enthusiasts heading for a brick wall, you'd yell out a warning, wouldn't you? But supposing he shouted back: "Don't bother me with brick walls. I'm a cyclist, not a brick-layer." You'd think the man a bit of a lunatic, wouldn't you? And why? Because brick walls are the concern of every man alive who wants to go on living.

And so is God, only very much more so. To think you can go through life disregarding the one who created life, your life, and for a special reason that concerns you — that's like beating your head against a brick wall and pretending it isn't there. That attitude, all too common today, is flying in the face of Truth, ignoring the whole purpose and meaning of Christ's life and death.

1

NO NEUTRAL MEN

"A sign of contradiction," was the phrase used by Simeon to predict the destiny of the Child he held in his arms. A sign that for the rest of time many would refuse to acknowledge. Some had already done so. "He came unto his own and his own received him not." For Simeon himself there was no doubt. "This is the Light that shall give revelation to the Gentiles. This is the glory of Israel."

When the Child grew to manhood he spoke of this persistent but unavailing hostility. Using another metaphor and referring to his Church, with which he identified himself, his Mystical Body, he gave the firm assurance that "the gates of Hell shall not prevail against it." But he implied that the struggle would be unending. He would draw all men to himself, only for some to reject him. "He that is not for me, is against me."

Does it not seem that this prophecy of our Lord, following that of Simeon and John, has not in fact been fulfilled? In our modern world, and particularly in this country of ours, are not the vast majority of people neither for nor against Christ, but merely indifferent? "When Jesus came to Brimingham they simply passed him by." Or as Carlyle wrote even of primly religious Victorian society: "If Jesus Christ was to come today, people would not even crucify him. They would ask him to dinner and hear what he had to say and make fun of it."

There lies the answer. To shrug off Christ and the claims of Christianity with a supercilious smile isn't indifference but rejection. In another context, this *pro* or *con* has been seen as a clear-cut choice by the leader of atheistic Communism, Christianity's bitterest enemy. Khrushchev stated categorically, there can be no neutral men.

Christ is the end, for Christ is the beginning.
Christ the beginning, for the end is Christ.

GOD MADE MAN

"What think ye of Christ?" Imagine yourselves in the crowds that rubbed shoulders with him in the streets, not yet knowing him as God. What would have been your impression of him? You can't help feeling that you'd have been quite at home and at ease with him, can you? But how enthralling to hear him speak, raising his hearers above the harshness and injustice of their little lives. "You're the salt of the earth. God hasn't forgotten you, even if men have. Don't go and spoil it all by forgetting him and the way he wants you to live."

And he'd explain God's commandments, not as a set of petty rules to catch men out, but as the Father's way of guiding them in what he knew was best for them. It was him they obeyed or disobeyed, not just rules. Sin isn't merely being mean and hurtful to one another, but to God who is our loving Father. We must all speak to him like that, as "Our Father."

Christ kept harping on forgiving as we hope to be forgiven, and not judging others merely because what they did looked wrong. That was commonsense and so true, like everything he said; often comforting and sometimes hard but it rang a bell every time. And then it wasn't just what he said, but the way he put it over, in everyday language that all could understand.

Here was a Man among men, like us in all save sin, which isn't a need of human nature but only serves to diminish it. That was the difference that made all the difference. A man without sin, perfect Man, because he was God made man.

3

THE NAME OF JESUS

"His name was called Jesus, which was called by the Angel before he was conceived in the womb." So St. Luke tells us (2: 21).

Shakespeare makes Juliet ask pertly, "What's in a name?" In fact, it's the most personal thing about us, expressing our individuality. All of us humans share our nature, what we are, but none of us can share it with anyone else. Even between identical twins, there's that something or other that makes you, you, and me, me, and that's our individual personality.

So back to the name. For most of us, it may not mean much, but it does to the famous and the infamous. Call somebody Caesar or Napoleon; Henry VIII or Hitler; Judas or Shylock or a Quisling, and we'll be in no doubt as to what we mean. So also if you speak of a woman as a Florence Nightingale or a Mother Teresa, you know with whom you are comparing your friend.

You and I are followers of Christ, whose name we've been taught to reverence from our childhood. "In the name of Jesus," wrote St. Paul to his first converts, "let every knee bow, of those in heaven, on earth and under the earth. Let every tongue confess that the Lord Jesus Christ is in the glory of God the Father."

In the sacred name of Jesus, Peter worked his first miracle.

Is that nothing but a name to us, or will we too let our Divine Lord work in our souls and our lives those miracles of grace that He is so ready to do?

4

THE HIDDEN LIFE

Christ became Man to redeem the world, yet he fades from the scene for thirty years, and then crowds into a meagre two and a half years the task he'd been sent by his Father to do.

Were the long, quiet years spent at Nazareth a waste of time? Of course not. But let's ask ourselves, why not? God had an overall plan for the redemption of mankind and every detail of Christ's life was part of that plan. How then does his hidden life fit into that plan? It must have a meaning. What is it? Man fell from God's favour by rebelling against God's authority. The first sin was, like every other sin, an act of disobedience rooted in pride.

God came to teach us that the only way back to God is by obedience rooted in humility. And so, as St. Paul says, he who was God, came to us in human form, accepting an obedience which brought him to death. Wasn't Christ always telling us that he came to do his Father's will, not his own? And he asked us to say that too, in our daily prayers: "Thy will be done on earth, as it is in heaven."

But no mere words make the same impact as the force of example, do they? Our Saviour knew that too and so, day in and day out, he practised what he was later to preach. The eloquent silence of 30 years is broken by one all-important sentence: "He went back with them to Nazareth and continued to be under their authority."

5

CHRIST'S LITTLE WAY

Consider the circumstances of Christ's birth among men. Everything seemed to have been left to chance. Mary did not tell Joseph. Bethlehem was the village foretold for his birth, yet Mary would never have gone there but for the census ordered from distant Rome. And when she got there, only just in time for Jesus' birth, no proper place could be found. He was born hurriedly in a stable, with a manger as a makeshift cradle.

Then for 30 years the Incarnate God lived in Nazareth, a backwater of Galilee, right off the main road, which went through Cana. It was a village of boorish, thick-headed farmers, laughed at by their fellow-countrymen. And there God lived and worked as a carpenter in a cottage no different from hundreds of others.

Then less than three years of public preaching up and down the countryside of only a part of the little country of Palestine. How incongruous it all seems: Palestine, a province of the Empire that the Romans looked on with contempt; Galilee which the Jews themselves despised; Nazareth which the Galileans spoke of with contempt; "Can any good come out of Nazareth?"

And Christ left the world apparently as unruffled as when he entered it; for the execution of a disturber of the peace, though it caused a nine-day wonder in Jerusalem, caused no stir in Rome. It was a mere matter of Jewish domestic politics in a turbulent but unimportant corner of the great Empire.

All this was the background of Christ's life and death among men, of the salvation of mankind. And the followers he deliberately picked to spread his message through the sophisticated Greco-Roman world were peasants and fishermen; illiterate, stubborn, cowardly — until his grace and the Holy Spirit of Truth got to work on them and they got to work on the world. Conquest by failure — by the weak and the poor. Triumph by martyrdom — that is the paradox of Christianity. "My ways are not your ways," saith the Lord.

THE OBEDIENCE OF CHRIST

Mary and Joseph play a vital part in God's plan to redeem the world. It is they who, as all parents do, exercise the authority of God over the child committed to their care.

What a unique privilege it was for Mary and Joseph to form the human mind of the divine Child entrusted to them by his eternal Father. With what loving care did they use the authority given them by God over his Son and theirs. Christ knew that, in obeying them, he was obeying the will of the Father, who was theirs as well as his. It was in his home that our Saviour, who came to redeem us all by obedience, first learnt to say the prayer that was always on his lips: "Thy will be done."

Can you see now all that the Hidden Life of Nazareth, no less than Bethlehem and Calvary, has its part to play in the redemption of the world? And what is the lesson of Nazareth for us? Parents have a privilege, and responsibility, akin to that of Mary and Joseph, in caring for the souls as well as the bodies of the children given them by God.

It is his divine authority that they exercise. And children in their turn must have the obedience and reverence that the Christ Child showed to Mary and Joseph. And in our families, as with the Holy Family, the bond between us all must be the bond of love — the love God has for each of us, our love for him, and the love we have for each other in him.

THE SERMON ON THE MOUNT

Sympathy, compassion, the capacity to enter into ordinary people's lives with gentle, loving understanding — that was the most striking and appealing characteristic of Christ. Take the Sermon on the Mount, for example. For an hour or more he spoke to the poor oppressed peasants of Palestine, huddled on the hill that runs up behind the little town of Capernaum.

They listened in silence, fascinated, as he made them forget their sordid lives — made them see how hardship could be counted a blessing; convinced them that they, the outcasts of the world, were still of great account in the eyes of God. As they listened to Christ, those men and women learnt for the first time that God loved them, and, more amazing still, he wanted them to love him.

That put sin in a new light — and a rather dingy, murky light — not only sins of the flesh that could break up a family's happiness, but sins of the spirit that could destroy a man's character — perjury, hypocrisy, deliberately damning a man for sins one committed oneself.

He gave them the most down-to-earth commonsense advice: "Do to other men all that you would have them do to you." He talked to them about their hot-tempered quarrels and showed them the blessings of reconciliation with each other and with God. He sympathized with them in all their daily cares, their worries about earning their living, and always he urged them not to fret, never to be over anxious, to do their best and trust in the providence of a loving God.

8

CHRIST AND THE HYPOCRITES

"Woe upon you, hypocrites," Christ stormed at the Scribes and Pharisees. Why did he round so mercilessly on these men, he who was so compassionate with sinners? It was because of what they pretended to be. They were trained in the Law of God and committed, in conscience, to teach it. Ordinary men and women trusted them to show the way to salvation, the will of God. Poor people, who looked for guidance to these men in the ways of God, were deliberately being misguided. That's why Christ denounced them for slamming the door of heaven in men's faces.

The poet Browning wrote: "It's a dangerous thing to play with souls and matter enough to save one's own." These men were toying with immortal souls by distorting the truth. You know what our Lord had to say about that: "There's no need to fear those who kill the body, but have no means of killing the soul. Fear him more, who has the power to ruin body and soul in hell. Woe to the world, for the hurt done to consciences."

But it wasn't only for the harm they were doing to others that Christ denounced the Pharisees. It was the fact that they were so utterly conceited and self-complacent. They considered themselves a class apart, a cut above others and expected everyone to bow down before them for laying down a Law which they didn't keep themselves. That's what our Lord pointed out at the beginning of his tirade; "Do what they tell you. Continue to observe what they tell you. But don't imitate their actions, for they tell you one thing and do another."

And that is hypocrisy.

9

CHRIST IN EVERYMAN

Christ has told us to see him, our crucified Saviour, thirsting on the cross, in everyone in need. And it is he who looks at us in gentle reproach when we refuse. To see Christ in our less fortunate fellow men and women — what a world of difference that would make to us, and to them, if we only remembered it. But we don't, because we hardly believe it. We know that Christ said so and, if we think about it at all, we admit it's a wonderful, idealistic thought, but like other things he said, such as turning the other cheek and so on, we decide it's not very practical.

We're ready enough to do our stint of Christian charity, but if we're honest with ourselves, it's more often than not a face-saving affair. We run into a down-and-out, slip him a quick coin to get rid of him and call that charity. We're always being appealed to for good causes. We dole out a donation and that's that. We visit the sick and aged poor and find them petulant and ungrateful. We come away, bored and irritated, glad when our visit's over.

What a chance we've missed not to remember and keep on reminding ourselves of Christ's golden words; "Whatever you do for the least of my brethren, you do it to me." Not just "for" me, but "to" me. He is there, present in our fellow men, as we believe him to be truly present in ourselves, spiritually, sacramentally.

Jesus Christ isn't a dead memory but a living reality, given us by his father and ours, to be with us always, here and hereafter.

10

THE GOOD SHEPHERD

Christ was all things to all men, for his mission was to bring salvation to all. Men's innermost thoughts were, and are, an open book to Jesus Christ. And the love of his sacred heart goes out with deepest compassion to those who most need sympathy and understanding, not only because of their sorrows but also because of their sins.

Christ never wasted time moralising on misfortune or passing pious platitudes on sinners. He was never negative. He always did something to lighten the lot of the unfortunate. Yet while he soothed and mended their stricken bodies, he never missed the chance to pour the balm of encouragement into their downcast souls. As his healing hand was laid upon them, he would say their sins were forgiven, or "Thy faith hath brought thee recovery."

He was always quick to show the broken in body and soul that they were worth something, not to other men, and maybe not in their own eyes, but they were to God who loved them, loved them so much that he sent his Son among them to prove his love. And it was the same among sinners. Christ never sought to prove them wrong, but neither did he gloss over their sins. He sought instead to show them that sin is simply good gone wrong, twisted round into the wrong turning. They were sheep that had gone astray, each into his own way. And he was the Good Shepherd sent to guide them back along the straight and narrow path.

THE GENIUS OF CHRIST

Our Lord had a genius for friendship. There was a fascination about him that none could resist, and he welcomed them all with open arms. This extraordinary personal devotion, this loving trust, that Jesus Christ inspired, is unique in the history of mankind. It has continued unabated for nearly 2,000 years, with the same enthusiasm, the same eagerness, to sacrifice all, even life itself, for a person who is as alive and real to his followers now as then. And the reason is, as St. Paul put it: "What Jesus Christ was yesterday and is today, he remains for ever."

The same thing was said eighteen centuries later by a surprising witness. The disillusioned Emperor Napoleon, his dream of conquest shattered, and with only death to await in a lonely island exile, at last faced the moment of truth. "What an abyss between my profound misery and the reign of Jesus Christ, preached, loved, adored and living in all the universe."

Christ, who rose from the grave, conquered death and is "ever-living to make intercession for us." When he, who is the Son of God, came to live among us as the Son of Man, he was never for one moment out of contact with his Eternal Father. He was always the link between God and Man, because he is both. And so, too, in returning to his Father, he has never lost contact with us. He is always the link between Man and God. We've never lost him; nor he us. He is always fulfilling his promise to be with us all days, even to the end of the world.

CHRIST, OUR TRUST, OUR HOPE

Today, perhaps more than ever before in human history, men are straining to see some meaning in life, because we've reached a point where human life could so easily be completely wiped off the face of the earth. Hundreds of submarines and rockets are constantly ready and can, with unprecedented speed, reach any target in the world with nuclear weapons, a single one of which contains an explosive power equal to that of all weapons used during the Second World War.

The unthinking say that if there is a God he won't allow it.

The unbeliever says there isn't a God, so he can't stop it.

We've heard something like that before somewhere. Remember the mockers on Calvary? "He trusted in God. Let God help him now." But God doesn't wipe out men who deny him. He says: "I will not the death of a sinner, but that he turn from his wicked way and LIVE."

Christ has the answer to the horrifying dilemma that faces mankind today. To those who threaten, from whatever motives, good or bad, to bring upon God's world a vast holocaust of mutual destruction, he gives a warning: "All those who take up the sword will perish by the sword."

To those of us who watch helplessly at this monstrous mockery of God and his gifts. Christ offers another weapon; the Sword of the Spirit: the weapon of prayer: "Father, forgive them, for they know not what they do." And the breastplate of salvation: Trust in God: "Father, into Thy hands I commend my spirit." Puny weapons, you feel? Yet they were enough to carry Christ from death to the life he calls us to share with him.

13

INTERCESSION TO MARY

All graces, like all natural gifts, come from God alone. And those graces have been won for us by our Mediator between God and Man; the Saviour who is both God and Man. All supernatural grace is conferred through Christ. Yet all members of his Mystical Body can mediate with the Mediator through the prayer of intercession; "Pray for one another that you may be saved," says the Apostle James.

The prayer of mutual intercession is the practical expression of the doctrine of the Communion of Saints, which all true Christians profess in the Creed. This exchange of prayer isn't something that ceases with this life, but continues after death. Amongst the prayers of all the Saints, whose can compare with those of the Blessed Mother of the Redeemer, so closely united to him in his earthly work at Bethlehem, Nazareth and Calvary, and now united with him in heaven?

As she was with him when he died, so will she watch over our deathbed, for do we not beg her every day of our lives "pray for us sinners now and at the hour of our death?" — those two all-important moments that are ever drawing closer and will one day coincide. So, with the boldness of St. Bernard, we refuse to believe that she will leave us unaided; and with the simple confidence of children, her children, we can say: "O Mary, you can't say you can't, and you won't say you won't. So you will, won't you?"

14

MOTHER OF SORROWS

Mary, the Mother of the Mystical Christ, united to the Redeemer in a closer, deeper sense than anyone else, co-operates in the Redemption in a unique way. Some part of our accepted suffering at least must be set against our own sins. But Mary had no sins at all, and so all she suffered could be wholly for the sins of mankind. That suffering began with her Motherhood and persisted throughout her life. We fittingly turn to her as the Mother of Sorrows, for she suffered, so to speak, in her own right and as our own representative, as the Prophet Simeon foretold: "This child is destined to be a sign which men will refuse to recognise. As for thy own soul, it shall have a sword to pierce it."

The sorrows and sufferings of the Mother of Sorrows have a value that derives from the passion of the Man of Sorrows: "If any man will come after me, let him deny himself, take up his cross and follow me." That command of the Saviour applied to his Mother as to the rest of us. She too had to deny herself in order to follow him, co-operate with him, as we all must, in the work of Salvation.

Yet her co-operation with him, her mediation and intercession for the whole of mankind stands apart from ours. We pray and offer our sacrifices through Christ our Lord; so does she, but she stands in a unique relationship to him, for of all creatures she is not only the servant of God, she is the Mother of God. And, of course, all Mary's glory, all her privileges, derive from that tremendous fact: she is God's Mother.

IMMACULATE CONCEPTION

On the Feast of the Immaculate Conception, we give thanks to God for her whom Wordsworth, in an inspired phrase, called "Our tainted Nature's solitary boast." St. Thérèse of Lisieux expressed this in one simple sentence: "To me she is much more a Mother than a Queen."

Of course, it is the Divine Motherhood of Mary that is her supreme glory and the justification for every one of the titles showered upon her in Catholic devotion. But this doesn't set her apart from us. Rather the opposite. In God's plan of Redemption, the mother of the second Adam had to be a descendant of the first. So Mary and the rest of us have the same family connections, and since, through her, Christ became our brother, we can say we're related to God "on his Mother's side."

Mary's Motherhood was unique in that the new Life conceived within her was brought about by the direct power of God. She shares the joys and anxieties of Motherhood with every mother the world over.

She knew the wonder of pregnancy as the Child grew within her.

She knew the bliss of nursing him at her own breasts.

Her loving eyes watched every move he made. Her gentle hands supplied his every need. It was she who taught him his first faltering steps and then, one wondrous day, heard his baby lips striving to speak; the Eternal Word of God using his first word as Man and calling to her as his Mother.

Like every other mother, Mary lived in and for her Son, and when the joy of Bethlehem turned into the bitterness of Calvary, she was still there to clasp him in her arms, the Blessed Mother.

MARY'S SINLESSNESS

Mary was truly saved by the merits of her Son, foreseen by Almighty God who transcends time. The effect of this foreseeing of the merits of the Redeemer by his Heavenly Father was that Mary's soul was preserved in the first moment of her existence from that original sin, which otherwise would have overtaken her as one of Adam's descendants.

The complete sinlessness of Mary was bestowed upon her, not for her own sake, but for the sake of her all-holy Child to whom she was to communicate her flesh and blood by the power of the Holy Spirit. Mary's sinlessness is part of the reverence due to God and one which, if we can use the expression, God owed himself.

The best statement I know of the place of Mary in the economy of our salvation and the reason for devotion to her, was made in a letter written in 1399 by Thomas Arundel, then Archbishop of Canterbury, to the Bishop of London and his other suffragans:

> The contemplation of the great mystery of the Incarnation, in which the Eternal Word chose the holy and immaculate Virgin that from her womb he should clothe himself with flesh, has drawn all Christian nations to venerate her from whom came the first beginnings of our redemption.

> But we English, being the servants of her special inheritance, and her own Dowry, as we are commonly called, ought to surpass others in the fervour of our praises and devotions.

Do we, these days? The Blessed Mother prophesied that "all generations shall call me blessed." Don't let ours be the first to fail her.

17

THE ANNUNCIATION

If you want to get somewhere in this world, to achieve name and fame, you've got to think big and act big, haven't you? It's no good fretting your heart out in some provincial backwater. You've got to go to Town; get in with the right people, get yourself talked about. Make a splash and you'll be carried along on the wave of success. That's roughly the way of the world, isn't it? Now let's look at the way of God.

The task God set himself was freedom of the human race from the bondage of sin, and this he aimed to do not by the use of divine force, but by the conquest of men's hearts by love. "God so loved the world that he gave up his only-begotten Son." And the first thing the Son of God did was to lay aside the splendour of his Godhead and become one of us.

He did this at a moment in history when the whole known civilised world was ruled by one State, the Roman Empire, at the height of its prestige and prosperity. That choice of time was God's only concession to man's ideas of the fitness of things. He came amongst us "in the fullness of time," as St. Paul puts it.

We would also have expected an equally careful choice of place and environment; in Rome, maybe, of an imperial mother with royal influence to further his teaching. But God chose for his mother a Jewish girl of sixteen, unknown outside her native town. "The Virgin's name was Mary." We know little more about her. And God even asked her consent to become the mother of his son, for his messenger, Gabriel, came not with a command but with God's proposal, which Mary did not understand. She was troubled. She asked questions. "She kept all these things, pondering them in her heart."

THE ASSUMPTION OF MARY

"The Assumption is an assumption" was the comment to me of a Protestant writer on November 1, 1950, when Pope Pius XII proclaimed as a dogma the taking into heaven of Mary, body and soul, at the end of her life on earth.

In a sense the man was right, for the Vicar of Christ, in exercising his Christ-given prerogative, was assuming a truth of Faith believed and devotionally practised since time immemorial by the People of God. For Mary was anticipated that resurrection of the body which, as we profess in our Creed, we too will enjoy at the end of time. (In a way the miracle of God's power, his re-creative power, will be more manifest in our case than Mary's, for our bodies will be raised from corruption and physical destruction which she did not undergo).

Whether Mary actually died has been left open to the speculation of theologians. Her exemption from sin did not necessarily prevent her from paying the common debt of humanity. Adam would have died in the course of nature, even if he had never sinned; and St. Augustine says that our Blessed Saviour would have died by the natural decay of old age, if he had not been done to death on Calvary. Still, even if the Virgin Mother tasted of death, her body was preserved, as was her Son's, from corruption, and it was united to her soul in Heaven. That has always been the belief of the true Christian. As Monsignor Knox said:

For myself, I have never doubted the doctrine of the Assumption. You see we think it the most natural thing in the world that body and soul should be separated after death. But it isn't a natural thing at all; soul and body were made for one another, and the temporary divorce between them is something extraordinary, occasioned by the Fall.

In our Blessed Lady, not born under the star of that defect, human nature was perfectly integrated; body and soul belonged to one another, as one day, please God, yours and mine will.

THE CHURCH IS CHRIST

The Catholic Church alone can trace her authority and commission, with certainty, back to a Divine Founder who said:

> As the Father hath sent me, I also send you . . . All authority in heaven and on earth has been given to me. You therefore, must go out, making disciples of all nations . . . teaching them to observe the Commandments which I have given you. And I am with you all days even to the end of the world.

It is because the Church is Christ and Christ is the Church that she has remained always essentially the same — in faith, in worship, in organisation and government. Development and growth there have been, of course, in Christ's Mystical Body, just as the physical Christ developed and grew from the inarticulate Babe of Bethlehem hidden away in a stable, to the Man of Calvary who preached to the whole world from the Tree of the Cross.

Christ's Church has continued to develop and grow as he prophesied she would, from the grain of mustard seed into the tree whose branches overspread the earth — a natural, organic growth, not the kind of monstrous development that consists in rejecting what you have previously believed or in believing today the opposite of what you believed yesterday. Can you think of a truth the Catholic Church once proclaimed and now denies? Or once denied and now proclaims?

All down the ages the Church, like the good teacher she was appointed by Christ to be, has been taking the truths revealed by Christ and patiently, but firmly, unfolding and explaining them so that her children may understand all that they mean.

THE PRIESTHOOD OF THE LAITY

Christ has asked us to live, here on earth, the life of God. By sharing our nature and redeeming it he has called us to union with him, to be sharers in the Godhead, as he was in our humanity. He calls us to this through the sacrament of Baptism, which he instituted as the means of giving sanctifying grace to our souls and thereby making us one with him, as members of his Mystical Body, the Church.

Moreover, this first sacrament of membership, of union with him, opens up the soul to the operation of the Holy Spirit, promised by Christ and sent to his Church and to all who belong to it. All that is the essential glory and privilege of being a Christian. It is the vocation that is common to all members of Christ's Mystical Body, which is his Church.

There is no distinction as between pope, bishop, priest or layman in what constitutes being a member of the Mystical Body of Christ and the privileges thereof, namely, union with Christ through whom we become Sons of God. All are called to equal membership and therefore to the same vocation. There is an idea, not uncommon though entirely wrong, that regards the Church as a kind of clerical closed-shop with bishops, priests, monks and nuns as full members, and the laity on the fringe, in a kind of associate membership, graciously allowed to participate in the Church's work, to a limited degree where they can be useful — like passing around the plate and filling it!

Of course you generously do that, but there are many other ways in which you can shape *your* priesthood with your ordained pastor.

21

WE ARE THE CHURCH

Christ's concern was with immortal souls. He didn't care where they assembled to hear him — on the mountainside, by the lake, in the synagogue or in the courtyards of the Temple. He drove home the lesson of his example by the precept of his word, commanding his apostles to go out and teach and promising his followers that: "Wherever two or three shall be gathered together in my name, there am I in the midst of them."

So that's how we always start — with a handful of the faithful assembled together (that's what the word "Church" means) in Christ's name, that is, gathered around an ordained, commissioned priest of Christ, to hear the word of Christ and live the life of Christ through the Mass and the Sacraments.

These Sacraments were instituted by Christ as outward signs of inward grace. As the grace of God enters the soul of each one of us by Baptism, so the body of each one of us becomes the temple of the Living God, the dwelling of the Blessed Trinity; when you and I were confirmed, our bodies housed the Holy Spirit. "Do you know," says St. Paul, "that you are the temples of God and that the Spirit of God dwells within you? The temple of God is holy and you are this temple."

Again, when we receive the Bread of Life in Holy Communion, our bodies become in an even more obvious way, a resting place for Christ, a new Crib of Bethlehem. So it is you and I who are the true tabernacles of God, the Church that He longs for far more than the temple made with hands, a thing of bricks and mortar.

22

THE MULTI-RACIAL CHURCH

The Church is a multi-racial and a multi-national Church. One of the most striking facts of the Second Vatican Council was the number of bishops of all races who assembled in the Eternal City. As a result of contacts established between bishops at the Council, many of the dioceses in the U.K. have entered into commitments to dioceses and ecclesiastical territories overseas, sending clergy, religious and lay people to help them.

While these overseas methods of mission work remain of absorbing interest, it is to be remembered that the missions are also on our door-steps. Many of the people who have benefited from the money we gave to missionaries are now living, working and studying in our midst. Over 50,000 students are over here in England from so-called mission countries. Many of these, even if not Christians, were educated in Christian schools by Christian missionaries. They were taught that God is the Father of us all and that as sons of God we are also brothers of one another in Christ. The tragedy is that many have received little experience of this from the Christian community in this country. Relatively few have been received into a British home. Some feel that our lack of welcome is because they are black and because we do not really accept them as equals and sometimes do not want to know them.

The Vatican Council teaches us the contrary: "Christ and the Church, which bears witness to him by preaching the gospel transcend every particularity of race or nation and therefore cannot be considered foreign anywhere or to anybody" (Missions: para 8).

But the realisation of our share in Christ's mission to the whole world should be evident first and foremost in our sense of mission for the people around us.

THE UGANDA MARTYRS

On 2 July, 1877, the first Christian Missionaries (Protestants) arrived in Uganda, in response to an appeal by the explorer, Henry Stanley, who had set out to find his fellow explorer and missionary. When they met in the wilds of Africa, Stanley greeted him with the now classically casual remark: "Dr Livingstone, I presume."

Catholics soon followed, led by Father Lourdel, known as 'Mapera' (mon père). In canonizing the twenty-two Martyrs of Uganda on 18 October 1964, Paul VI said:

> This was a field of missionary apostolate where ministers of the Anglican confession, Englishmen, came first. They were followed two years later by Catholic missionaries. Not only Africa but civilisation itself ought to remember them as among its most distinguished men.

Today, a century since the gospel came to Uganda, the country is 63 per cent Christian. How did it come about that Catholicism, preached by Frenchmen, overtook Protestantism in a British colony, where it arrived first? The first African Bishop, Kiwanuka, said: "Catholicism spread fast because all the Blessed Martyrs of Uganda laid a solid foundation for their lay apostolate by leading perfect and exemplary Christian lives."

There are two lessons for post-Vatican II European Catholics to learn from Christian Uganda. The first is that the Church's success has been due to the close collaboration that has always existed between laity and clergy. The second is that, when we recall that the ashes of the twenty-two Catholic Martyrs were mixed with those of the Anglican Martyrs, we should realise that Uganda has a special ecumenical message for the Church of today.

THE SO-CALLED WEALTH
OF THE CHURCH

The vast wealth of the Church is an easy target for attack. Much of this so-called wealth is vested in buildings; the magnificent cathedrals and churches that sprang up all over Europe, including our own country, where, since the Reformation, they have passed out of our hands.

One should remember that these masterpieces of architecture were raised to the glory of God by rich royalty and nobility who, even when seeking to leave to posterity a memorial of themselves, nevertheless gave employment and a livelihood to a vast number of artisans and artists. The creations of their genius have become the heritage of mankind, not the possessions of prelates and priests.

To secularise, that is to nationalise, famous cathedrals, as has been done in Russia, would do as little for the poor, as the selling of the contents of our National Gallery or the British Museum would do to solve the housing problem in the slums of London.

It isn't the material wealth of the Church, in terms of brick and mortar and artistic treasure, that is in question, but the attitude of the Church's servants, pope, prelates and priests, to material well-being. Most priests in this country live in a state of comparative affluence, at least equal to, if not above, that of the average of their parishioners. But there are many who don't and they are not, by and large, those who serve working-class town parishes, but priests in so-called "one-horse" missions, covering wide areas in the country but a small Catholic population.

THE EVER-RENEWING CHURCH

Our Western way of life is basically a Catholic Christian thing. It is the product of the greatest achievement in history, when the early Church salvaged the decaying ruins of Greek culture, of Roman law and government, then took the vigorous, lusty but lawless barbarian by the scruff of the neck, so to speak, and proceeded to apply to all three the principles and standards of the Catholic ideal, thereby laying the foundations of a Europe essentially Christian in its character and outlook. As Sir Arnold Lunn remarked: "There is no aspect of our modern life which has not, at some period, passed through the mould of the Catholic Church."

And yet the Church's task in welding together our Western civilisation has been, and always will be, the triumph of failure. As Chesterton put it so characteristically:

> Christendom has had a series of revolutions and in each one of them Christianity has died many times and risen again, for it had a God who knew the way out of the grave. Europe has been turned upside down over and over again . . . and at the end of each of these revolutions the same religion has again been found on top. The Faith is always converting the age, not as an old religion, but as a new religion. At least five times the Faith has to all appearances gone to the dogs. In each of these five cases it was the dog that died.

In every crisis the Church has pulled herself together, renewed her strength and come forth rejuvenated, galvanized into new life. The Church is "like the Mississippi — it just keeps rolling along . . . Let it roll in full flood, inexorable, irresistible, benignant, to broader lands and better days."

OUR MISSIONARY VOCATION

All baptised Christians share in the mission of the Church. We are all missionaries, for better or worse, in our daily lives and contacts. As members of the living Christ, all the faithful have been incorporated into him and made like unto him through baptism, confirmation and the Eucharist.

Hence all are duty bound to co-operate in the expansion and growth of his body, so that they can bring it to fullness as soon as possible. How can we fulfil this obligation to work for the spread of the faith and the building up of Christ's body? The first thing is to be concerned about the mission of the Church. Each must realise that his first and most important obligation towards the spread of the faith is this: to lead a profoundly Christian life.

All of us are surrounded by people who are in some sense strangers, to us, to each other and to Christ. All these need the missionary love of Christ. Most of us find it difficult to be really open with strangers and newcomers. Many of us don't have the energy or even interest to be bothered with people outside the family circle or our own inward looking group.

The missionary activity of the Church is an outflowing of charity. As Pope Paul VI said: "Even before converting the world, we must meet the world and talk to it."

When we receive Christ at Mass, let us ask him to make us like himself, ready to commit ourselves to becoming more open to strangers. Then the Church will appear "as a sign lifted up among the nations," the "Light of the World" and the "Salt of the Earth."

UPON THIS ROCK

Christ delegated his divine authority on all matters necessary for salvation, in faith as in morals, to a fisherman called Simon Johnson (Simon Bar Jona), whom he re-named Peter, the Rock, because it was he who, first of all his disciples, proclaimed his Master's divinity: "Thou art the Christ, the Son of the living God."

That Simon Peter did so was an act of faith that went far deeper than the impact Christ's dynamic humanity had had upon him. "Flesh and blood has not revealed this to thee, but my Father who is in heaven." So Peter, the Rock, was given the Keys of Christ's Kingdom.

Again when the rest, puzzled as were those who left Christ, by the Saviour's promise to be with them, as the Bread of Life, it was Peter who refused even to contemplate giving up his allegiance: "Lord to whom shall we go? Thou hast the words of eternal life."

Yet he did, in a moment of cowardice, forswear his Master but quickly repented with a threefold affirmation of love: "Lord, thou knowest all things. Thou knowest that I love thee." For that Peter was confirmed as Shepherd of Christ's flock: "Feed my lambs, feed my sheep." And he was given the most wonderful of all guarantees, a divine and therefore unfailing promise: "I have prayed for thee that thy faith fail not and that thou, being converted, confirm thy brethren."

Christ's promise to Peter is the heritage of those who have succeeded him in his divine charge, to be Christ's Vicar, as it happens (it could have been otherwise) in the bishopric (or Christian community) of Rome — the Pope.

I'm the Pope's man, because I'm Peter's man, because I'm Christ's man. How can the true Christian be anything else?

28

OUR HISTORIC TRIBUTE

Peter Pence, the contribution made once every year by the faithful to the direct support of Peter's successor, is of particular interest to us in England for it was our forefathers who started it.

The conversion of the Anglo-Saxons was the first mission organised and directed personally by a Pope, St. Gregory the Great. For that reason they regarded themselves as united, in a special way, to the Holy Father and the Holy See and very early on began making pilgrimages to Rome.

By the end of the 8th century, the growing number of Anglo-Saxons journeying to Rome resulted in the foundation there of a kind of pilgrims' hostel with its own church. For the support of the hostel, King Ine imposed on every family in Wessex a tax of one penny called Romscot to be paid "to St. Peter and the Church of Rome." It was abolished by Henry VIII in 1534, revived by Mary Tudor and finally suppressed by Elizabeth I in 1558.

The modern revival of Peter Pence took place after Pius IX was forced to flee to Gaeta in 1849 and in 1860 the greater part of the Papal States were seized. As an expression of sympathy for the exiled and impoverished Pope, contributions flowed in from all sides, even from Protestants, and a special Peter Pence office was opened in the Vatican for the administration of these funds by Pope Leo XIII in 1878.

We in England should be proud that through the historic tribute called Peter Pence, we were the first to enable the Servant of the Servants of God (the Pope's proudest title, first used by St. Gregory the Great) to use "the money of the poor for the benefit of the poor."

29

OBEDIENCE TO THE CHURCH

Papal encyclicals, as such, make no pretensions to be infallible — though they can be, if the Pope so wishes and makes his intentions clear. Yet, even short of that, they are an exercise in the Church's Christ-given magisterium, or teaching office, by the Vicar of Christ. He uses an encyclical letter as a medium of communication for matters of supreme importance for the well-being and instruction of the People of God. He may warn us against danger to the Faith within the Church or of attacks from outside, as Pope Pius XII did. He may stress the basic rights of Man, as in the great social encyclicals of Leo XIII, Pius XI, John XXIII and Paul VI.

Whatever the subject-matter, it is put before us by the highest authority the Church can offer, short of an infallible decree, and so requires of all, from bishops, clergy and laity, an obedient acceptance, an internal as well as an external assent.

On the authority of those papal statements, Pius XII wrote in 1950:

> Nor must it be thought that what is expounded in encyclical letters does not itself demand consent, on the pretext that in writing such letters the popes do not exercise the supreme power of their teaching authority. For these matters are taught with the ordinary teaching authority, of which it is true to say: He who heareth you, heareth me.

At Vatican Council II, in the Constitution on the Church, all the Bishops agreed and proclaimed that

> Religious submission of will and mind must be shown in a special way to the authentic teaching authority of the Roman Pontiff, even when he is not speaking *ex cathedra*. That is, it must be shown in such a way that his supreme magisterium is acknowledged with reverence, the judgments made by him are sincerely adhered to, according to his manifest mind and will.

ADVENT: THREEFOLD
COMING OF CHRIST

"There are three distinct comings of the Lord," said St. Bernard. "His coming to men, his coming into men, his coming against men."

The spiritual life is a constant renewal, simply because it is life, and all life demands replenishment. The soul, the spiritual part of man's mind, needs the stimulant of spiritual ideas, to foster and develop its life; and the soul, christened in baptism, must allow its life to be constantly renewed by Christ whose mystical life it shares.

That is why, throughout each year, the panorama of Christ's life is again unfolded before us. Whatever our age, we're no different from the children we were at school. We learn by repetition. And, that we may learn to value the golden heritage that is ours, we are urged each Advent, not to take Christ for granted, but to imagine ourselves without him, waiting, hoping.

His coming to men was that he might come into men. Holy Communion is a fulfilment of his will and his purpose in coming to us. It is also a renewal of that life, that spiritual nourishment our souls need. By all means make each Christmas Communion a special renewal of your soul's life, and an extra warm welcome to him, but don't let it be an isolated one.

Christ's coming against men, of which St. Bernard speaks, will be as our Judge, as he himself foretold. And how can he come against you, if you have let him all your life be with you, so that your soul lives of his life, your mind thinks his thoughts and your actions are his deeds?

CHRISTMAS: LIGHT OF LIGHT

Glory to God in high heaven — and on earth?

What utter contrast there was between the proclamation of Christ's coming and the reality; between the splendour of God's heralds and himself.

There in the hills above Bethlehem, the silence and the darkness, both symbols of a world without the Word who came to enlighten the world, were suddenly broken by the angels of light, singing their hymns of praise to God's glory. Night had been turned into day by the brightness of the King's messengers. What then would the Prince of Peace himself be like?

In excited expectation the shepherds hurry down from the hillside and there they find him, the Light of the World in the darkness of the stable — a new-born babe like any other. His mother a young Jewish girl no different from the rest, save for the light of love that her new motherhood had brought to her eyes.

No heavenly hymn but the inarticulate cry of the Word made Flesh, but in that sound they recognised the voice of God made Man, maker of the starry skies they knew so well; Lord and Master of the celestial choir they had just heard. They saw him, they knew him with the eyes of faith, and the words they murmured as they knelt before him were the first act of faith in the Saviour of Mankind. "Flesh and blood have not revealed it but my Father who is in Heaven."

Like the shepherds, you will recognise him with the insight of faith. Take him to your hearts and he will take you to his.

CHRISTMAS: PEACE ON EARTH

At Christmas time we wish each other happiness. God's wish for man is peace — "Peace on earth to men of goodwill . . ."

That first Christmas greeting echoed down from heaven to earth the night Christ our saviour, he whom the prophet called the Prince of Peace, left the glory of God in the Highest and came to live the life of man in its humblest, weakest, tenderest, most helpless form; the life of a babe to test the faith and love of mankind.

When the Divine Babe had grown to manhood and men of ill will were hounding him to his death, his last message was the same as the first, but this time he spoke it himself and explained it to his faithful few: "Peace I leave with you; my peace I give unto you, but not as the world giveth do I give unto you."

Every Christmas our hearts are grieved by the seeming mockery of God's message of peace. The guns are still barking. Brother still kills brother. Why? Because men are fighting to make a peace without goodwill.

The world needs more than ever the peace of Christ — a peace founded in charity — the love that looks on God and sees a Father; that looks on fellow men and sees that all are children of God and therefore brothers one to another.

Only through God, with God and in God can true peace be made. As we listen to God's Christmas Blessing: "Peace on Earth," let us search our own hearts, make our peace with God in Christ, and preach by the example of charity, forgiveness and goodwill to all around us, the peace that came down to earth that first Christmas night.

CHRISTMAS: THE REWARD
OF GOODWILL

The reward of goodwill is peace: peace within the family and a personal peace within the soul of each, for each is at peace not only with his brother in God, but with the Father of all. The result of this two-fold peace, family peace and individual peace, peace from within and peace from without, is a sincerity and a contentment that make up what we call happiness — the happiness of each other with one another and the happiness of each within his own soul. All that comes to those wise enough to show goodwill towards each other.

Mankind is yearning, as never before, for that true peace which is founded on goodwill: that readiness to look on God and see him as a Father. So tremendous a truth is obvious, save to those blinded by ill will. That is why the Peace of Christ was, and is, promised only to men of goodwill.

The gentle cry of the Babe in the manger, like the piteous cry of the Man on the Cross, was a clarion call to mankind for a return of mutual goodwill. At the first Christmas, that cry was answered by those who heard it with all their hearts as well as with their ears. They were the shepherds who came down from their hilltop to find the Good Shepherd of their souls, and the Wise Men who came from afar to discover Wisdom incarnate.

From that day to this there have been only two classes of people who heard the cry of Christ and found him with his message of peace: very simple souls and very wise minds, for only the very simple and the very wise can ever fathom the mystery of the manger.

NEW YEAR: ANYTHING NEW?

"Behold I make all things new." Anything new brings with it its own excitement, whether of joy or foreboding. The mood of expectation, love of surprise, eager looking forward to new experiences, new things, new people — only the cynic would call that childish, though it's certainly child-like, because to a child everything is new and it's part of a child's nature to want to learn.

The adult mind is no different. We're always searching, learning, never wholly content with what we have and hold and know, always stretching out to the unknown. God has made us that way because He alone can, and will, eventually satisfy all our longings. "Thou hast made us for thyself and our heart is restless till it rest in thee" (St. Augustine's words).

So it's natural to welcome the New Year, simply because it is new. Maybe also because we've good reason for relief that the past is over and done with.

I'm inclined to think King Solomon was steeped in a mood of disillusionment when he wrote: "Age succeeds age, and the world goes on unaltered . . . There can be nothing new, here under the sun."

We are learning almost daily that there's a lot that's new under the sun (and the moon) that we didn't know before. God meant it that way. He gave man a mind in the image of his own, intelligent, and also inquisitive, which God can never be, as he knows all.

So it's God's will that all his creatures work together to reveal the wonders of his creation and give praise to God's creative mind. Every piece of new knowledge about God and every New Year bring us nearer to the time when we shall not merely know about God but know him in himself.

NEW YEAR: MAKING RESOLUTIONS

Have you ever made, do you still make, resolutions? We used to, didn't we? And if you're like me you don't much want to be reminded of them. They didn't last, did they? Certainly mine didn't. Whether it was New Year or Lent, what I'd resolved to do, or not to do, was all too soon a broken promise. (It was Swift who said that promises are like pie-crusts, made to be broken.)

Resolutions "to do or not to do" are good, but they've got to be carefully worded, so as not to put you off and depress you, when you break them. That is why, in making resolutions, you should avoid using the words "Never" and "Always." You can see why, can't you. You say you are *never* going to do this (let's say smoke another cigarette). You do and your resolution has gone for a burton. You resolve *always* to be charitable to so-and-so under provocation. You say what you think, and that too has gone with the wind.

Now let me tell you of a resolution that you *can't* break. Whatever you resolve to do or not to do, simply say (1) *I will try hard* (which means that one slip-up won't put you off. You'll have another go). (2) *By the grace of God.* As St. Paul tells us, God always gives us grace enough to cope with any temptation, as long as we are ready to co-operate. (3) You must be *specific* in your resolution: to do or not to do this or that.

Resolutions are concerned with self-discipline. So don't expect too much of yourself.

As Samuel Butler wrote:

> *Great actions are not always true sons*
> *Of great and mighty resolutions.*

EPIPHANY: FAITH AND ACTION

"Hitch your wagon to a star." Three men, rich in wealth and wisdom, once did that and found God. Not quite where or how or what they expected, but they found him just the same. The idea for their search came from a firm faith that God was to be found somewhere.

But the moment they took their eyes off their star, following their own guess, instead of God's guidance, they lost the trail.

Surely, they thought, the Prince of Peace would be found in a King's palace, but there was no sign or knowledge of him in Jerusalem. So they thought back to God's word that they had read and the star was there again, leading them to God hidden away in a stable, nestling in His mother's arms. How incongruous their own royal robes and costly gifts must have seemed as they stepped through the straw.

In the story of the Magi you can read a parable of life, of your own quest for God. Faith is your starting point, faith which, though grounded in God's word and helped by His Church's teaching, is itself a gift of God, a gift which He will not deny you if you have the will to believe. As St. Ambrose says: "He who seeks faith already possesses it."

Yet Faith alone is not enough. You can have a flat-footed Faith, that stands still and does nothing. Your believing mind needs to be stirred into action by your will, a will buoyed up by Hope, and hope with God as its object.

Your search for God is a combination of Faith, Hope and Love, each intertwined with the others by a starry-eyed optimism that, however arduous your road, it will lead you to Bethlehem.

LENT: ITS MEANING

Lent, for Christians of all sorts — not just Catholics — is a time of prayer, especially the prayer of repentance, of sorrow for our sins.

In the early days of Christianity, Christians confessed their sins publicly, and did long public penance for them. As a sign of their sorrow and repentance, they went to Church and knelt, while the bishop poured ashes on their heads. Nowadays, we confess our sins privately, but we still go to church on Ash Wednesday to show that we are all sinners, and yet are ready to make up for past lapses, by prayer, fasting, and acts of charity.

So in church on Ash Wednesday, the priest sprinkled ashes on his head as a sign of his own sins, and then he marked each one of us with the sign of the Cross in ashes. As he did this, he may have said: "Remember! You are dust, and unto dust you shall return." Those words reminded us of death — a fact we all have to face. Not that we are morbid about it — why should we be? We know that death is only the bridge that leads us to a new life where God awaits us. Death isn't an enemy but a friend; it's not a sleep but an awakening; not a dream, but the great reality. It's not the end of everything, but the beginning of a new life with God, happier than anything we have known here on earth.

Death is God's call to us. When and how he will call us, he alone knows. But call he will. It's surely common-sense then to get to know something of God, to be on speaking terms with God in prayer, so that when the call comes we do not meet as strangers.

LENT: PENANCE

From time immemorial the Church has commended three main ways of self-discipline, which we know as "doing penance." They are prayers, alms deeds and fasting. World War II put an end to the old Lenten fast and now we simply top-and-tail Lent by fasting and abstinence on Ash Wednesday and Good Friday. A fairly recent innovation has been the one-day Family Fast.

This is an excellent idea for several reasons. It's both a family affair and a voluntary decision of each member what to give up, whether it's some food, drink, tobacco, sweets (in the case of the child) or anything else (such as a paper or a magazine) that you feel like buying on that day but don't. The savings we pass on, as a family, to those in greater need than ourselves.

All that is excellent, but in practice the amount any of us can save by self-denial on one day can't come to much in terms of cash. We should have more Family Fast Days or we should constantly keep CAFOD in mind by putting our hands in our pockets and not keep them there. That (and other needy causes) would take care of the second of the Church's recommendations: alms deeds. It's understandable that all of us, priests as well as people, get fed-up (or should it be browned-off?) with constant appeals and special collections, while at the same time the cost of living is always rising, so that we have that much less cash to spare for good causes.

But really all of us have something to share. There's little or no merit in giving unless we feel the pinch ourselves.

LENT: STATIONS OF THE CROSS

The Church urges more prayer upon us during Lent, because, as Our Lord reminded us, "You ought always to pray."

These weeks that lead to the liturgical renewal of the Pascal mystery are a time when we should make greater efforts to give our minds and hearts to God in prayerful reflection on all that our Divine Redeemer did for our eternal salvation. By his sufferings, his death and his rising to a new life are a warranty that we, too, can be united with him. To remind us of all this the Church gives us special daily Masses throughout Lent, (though the collects badly need re-writing).

A prayer that does apply very much to our preparation for Holy Week is the Way of the Cross. The "Stations" were thought up by the Franciscans, guardians still of the Holy Places in Jerusalem, as a means of enabling us all to join in spirit with our Saviour on his journey to Calvary, and of bringing home to our minds, through picture and prayer, the depth and reality of God's love for us, for you and for me.

Isn't that what Christianity is all about? Its very heart-beat? God loves us (as creator he could not do otherwise; God cannot not love) and, mystery of mysteries, longs for our love in return. Let us give it, without reservation, without argument. The Second Vatican Council has led to a lot of rethinking, but its primary object was re-loving, a spiritual renewal in the lives of us all. As St. Thérèse wrote: "There is only one thing to do on earth and that is to love Jesus, and to want other souls to love him too."

LENT: SHOW REPENTANCE

Penance and penitence, the two words should mean the same, but in our Catholic usage there has always been a distinction with a difference. The acceptance and fulfilment of penance by the individual should arouse in us penitence, a genuine internal change of heart, greater love towards God, of which the outward sign is the doing of an external act. But we all know the temptation to feel that having "done" our penance (whether it's the sacramental prayer or some deed of self-denial) we've done enough to make "satisfaction" to God. But have we?

So it is with God (and the Church which represents him). To keep the rules of the Church, recognising that they represent God's will for us, is a good thing. But we must do this, not just as an act of obedience but out of love of God, and sorrow for disobeying him. That's the whole difference between penance and penitence.

The penitential discipline of the Church (expressing God's will) has changed gradually and steadily down the ages. To begin at the end, the Friday Abstinence has gone. The daily Lenten Fast (a genuine penance, yet not all that tough) has been reduced to Ash Wednesday and Good Friday.

So be it. The ball is back in our court. Neither the Pope nor our Bishops have ever suggested that we don't need to do penance. On the contrary, our penances must be self-chosen acts of self-control which express for every one of us (and probably differently for each individual) a penitential turning away from our particular waywardness towards a genuine desire to show love of God through service of our neighbour.

41

LENT: PAIN WITHOUT LOVE

Pain suffered without love is purposeless. It can make you bitter, hateful to yourself, resentful. What a waste that is! But to suffer with love in your heart, with humble acceptance — that transforms the evil of pain into something noble, sacrificial. By calling upon you to take up your cross and follow him, Christ is offering you the golden opportunity to add your sacrifice to his, to give your pain, however small, however great, a redemptive value. That is what St. Paul meant when he said:

> The sufferings of Christ overflow into our own lives, but there is overflowing comfort, too, which Christ brings us. We must share his sufferings, if we are to share his glory. I consider that the sufferings of this present time are not worth comparing with the glory that is to be revealed to us.

I sometimes think there's a kind of law of compensation running through human history whereby, in the scales of justice, evil is counterbalanced by a corresponding measure of good; the selfishness of sin is offset by the sacrifice of self; hatred and cruelty must be met by love and compassion; contempt of God by obedience to God.

If that is so, then all that you suffer, whether it's a headache or a heartache, takes on a new meaning and gives you a new responsibility. If you turn away from the cross, you're turning your back on Christ. It is the world's tragedy that so many try to do both. They live — and die — without Christ, yet they cannot live — or die — without the bitterness of the cross, and the cross without Christ is a curse.

LENT: SPIRITUAL HEALTH

It is impossible to drift effortlessly into Heaven. St. Thomas More put the point to his children in his quiet, whimsical way: "You can't get to Heaven on a feather bed," he told them.

We must go back to St. Paul for a forceful metaphor that should appeal to this sport-loving age as it appealed to his audience of Corinthian athletes. He told them: "I so fight, not as one beating the air. I chastise my body and bring it into subjection." None of your clever sparring or shadow boxing for St. Paul. He begins his bout with his own body, so that it may obey his will. For, he says — and this is the most important point of all — "Everyone that striveth for the mastery refraineth from all things: and they indeed that they may receive a corruptible crown; but we an incorruptible one."

In dealing with God we need more of the sporting spirit of the athlete, the willingness to go into training, to order our spiritual lives in such a way that we become fit, healthy citizens of Heaven. Gone are the days when the Church harried us in her solicitude for our welfare. She leaves the ordering of our lives very largely to ourselves. We can pass as respectable Catholics and live lives of slackness and habitual venial, if not mortal, sin.

In the lives of all of us there is something to be ordered and controlled by careful training of the will and prayer for the strength that grace alone can give us. Let each choose for himself what it shall be.

LENT: ONLY ONE WAY

"If any man will come after me, let him deny himself and take up his cross and follow me."

We shun Christ's call because we cannot understand it. Does not the Gospel tell us that Christ died as a ransom paid once and for all on behalf of our sins — he the innocent for us the guilty? Is he not the Lamb of God who takes away the sins of the world? Of course, but in becoming a victim for our sins, he did not take away our sinfulness, and there lies the whole point. Our sacrifice, our renunciation, must follow that of Christ. We too must pass through the crucible of suffering before God can mould us to his will.

There is the answer to our puzzlement, our puzzlement at pain and cruelty, which is expressed so starkly in the threat of war which hangs over us as a constant threat.

There is the answer to what is otherwise unanswerable: the burden of the mystery of all this unintelligible world. Everywhere there is a sense of frustration that shackles us. We seek escape in pleasure, but find it a sorry will-o'-the-wisp.

The only key to the problem of the world's pain, the only real touch-stone of all human values is self-renunciation, self-sacrifice, the cross. It was the Saviour's only answer to his bewildered friends: "Ought not Christ to have suffered these things and so enter into His glory?" He also said: "The servant is not greater than his Master." For no human creature, whatsoever his condition or his belief, can there be any escape from suffering and from its penalty: Death. Ought we not therefore to suffer with Christ if we hope to enter with him into his Glory?

For the Christian, no less than for Christ, for you and for me as it was for him, the path of Calvary is the only way home to God.

GOOD FRIDAY: SUFFERING

"Father, into thy hands I commend my spirit." His soul returns to the Father, but his body hangs upon the cross for all to see. His body still hangs upon the cross as a reminder of all that he accomplished for us.

It is the crucifix, not just the cross, that makes true Christians. It is the crucifix alone that gives meaning to the pain of the world. When sorrow or suffering of mind or body come your way, as come they must, sooner or later, if you are stricken with pain or ill-health, your heart broken by a sudden tragic loss or the sight of suffering in one you love, if you are left lonely or desolate or find yourself the innocent victim of false accusers, if your lot is one of hardship or want — then you can do one of two things.

You can let yourself become embittered by the uselessness, the injustice of it all, but your problem will still be unsolved; it will still have no meaning for you.

Or you can see in your sorrow the cross that Christ asks you to carry with him. You can be a Simon of Cyrene, but a willing one. You can give your pain a redemptive value, as Mary did beneath the cross. Like her, you can help Christ in the salvation of souls, the souls of others as well as your own.

Christ showed his unmeasured love by dying to redeem us. It is only when we first share his sufferings and unite ours with his that we are able to enter with him into his glory.

GOOD FRIDAY: VICTORY OF DEATH

The crucifix must always be a dread reminder of the price our Saviour paid to redeem us from our sins. St. Thomas More calls upon us to let it always be a salutary warning against future betrayal.

When fierce temptations threat thy soul with loss,
Think on his Passion and the bitter pain,
Think on the mortal anguish of the Cross,
Think on Christ's blood let out at every vein,
Think of his precious heart all rent in twain.
For thy redemption think all this was wrought,
Nor be that lost which he so dearly bought.

Nature is normally indifferent to human tragedy. The sun will shine, while hearts are broken at the sight of suffering. Birds will sing in the trees while men lie dead and women weep. Flowers will deck a graveside in a riot of colour and scent. But on one unique occasion, Nature made protest at the greatest crime in history.

From noon onwards the sun was darkened; and there was darkness over all the land until three in the afternoon . . . and all at once, the veil of the sanctuary was torn this way and that from the top to the bottom and the earth shook, and the rocks parted asunder.

But soon the earth was to tremble again, this time with joy as the dead Saviour rose from the tomb.

I know that my Redeeemer liveth,
I see Him and I know that I have found
The long-delaying, long-expected Spring,
The strength to soar is in my spirit's wing.
For life is full of a triumphant sound,
And Death can only be a little thing.

A little thing? For "Death is swallowed up in victory," the victory of Life and Love triumphant.

EASTER: IF CHRIST BE NOT RISEN

Mary became the mother of Christ in the joy of Bethlehem. She began the task that will last until the end of time, the mothering of the Mystical Body of Christ. The Son achieved his labour of love through the only prayer with which to live: "Father, Thy will be done." And, as he turned back home, he left to us the only prayer with which to die: "Father, into thy hands I commend my spirit." His soul returned to his Father. But his body hung on the Cross for all to see.

In death, his Sacred Heart, laid open by the lance, showed his abounding love for each and all of us. Then the tragedy of Good Friday turned into the triumph of Easter Day. "Death is swallowed up in victory." But supposing it hadn't? What if Calvary had been the end of the story?

A Man of Sorrows, acquainted with infirmity, but an inspiration and a challenge to all that is best in the human heart and mind for the priceless precepts and counsel he proclaimed for all men of all time. If he were only that, it would still be much. "Ah, Christ, if there were nought hereafter, it still were best to follow thee!" And yet compelling as was the example of the perfect man to live it, if that were all, Christ would have failed us.

First in our faith: "If Christ be not risen again," wrote St. Paul, "then is our preaching vain and our faith also vain." Next, in our hope: "If in this life only we have hope in Christ, we are of all men most miserable."

Of two things only you and I are certain: We live. We must die. The Saviour too was a man who lived and died and then rose from the dead to prove that a life such as his could conquer death.

47

EASTER: TRIUMPH OVER SIN

The tragedy of Christ's life was that none, save his mother, understood his death. And the tragedy of so many, even of Christ's followers, was and is, failure to grasp the significance of the cross, seeing it only as a regrettable prelude to the triumph of the Resurrection, not as an integral part of the whole economy of Man's salvation planned and willed by God, carried through to its last harrowing details by the God-Man, who came to free man from the bondage of sin and was prepared to pay the price of sin — the sacrifice of his own life.

The Christ who rose from death to a new life is the Christ who was crucified. The Resurrection was a triumph over death. The Crucifixion was a triumph over sin. And it is because mankind has lost its sense of sin that the Crucifixion was, and is, seen as a lamentable failure in an otherwise triumphant life — a failure that could and should have been avoided if Christ's glorious message, the Good Tidings of the Gospel, was to have the universal success it deserved.

"Too slow of will, too dull of heart, to believe all those sayings of the prophets? Was it not to be expected that the Christ should undergo sufferings, and so enter into his glory?" And as he explained, they began slowly to understand and they went out triumphantly into an incredulous world to teach the lesson they had so painfully learned themselves.

"What we preach," Paul cried, "is Christ crucified. To the Jews, a stumbling-block, to the Gentiles mere folly; but to us who have been called, Jew and Gentile alike, Christ the power of God, Christ the wisdom of God."

EASTER: MY LORD AND MY GOD

Easter Day turned the tragedy of Good Friday into triumph. "Death is swallowed up in victory." But supposing it hadn't? What if Calvary had been the end of the story? It would still be much. "Ah, Christ, if there were nought hereafter, it still were best to follow thee!" And yet, compelling as was the example of the perfect life as God meant man to live it, if that were all, Christ would have failed us. "If Christ be not risen again, then is our preaching vain and your faith also in vain."

Of two things only I am certain: I live, I must die. The Saviour too was a Man who lived and died and then rose from the dead to prove that a life such as his could conquer death. His victory gives us a third certainty; an assurance of life after death for all who strive to live his life before death.

There was no understanding of this in the minds of the Apostles. That is why they couldn't believe their eyes and ears, when he appeared through closed doors and spoke to them. The answer to that was easy: "Give me to eat." Solid food isn't eaten by a ghost, still less by a figment of the imagination. And the test for Thomas was to touch his wounds and with that to confess the divinity of the Risen Christ: "My Lord and my God."

Those words we echo by custom at the Consecration of the Mass, where, with no benefit of sight or touch, our faith has the added blessing of resting on his word alone: "Blessed are those who have not seen and yet have learned to believe."

EASTER: THE EMPTY TOMB

"I know that my Redeemer liveth." Christ's resurrection is to be accounted a fact, not of hysteria but of history.

They had taken the lifeless body from the cross and buried it in the tomb. And that, for them, was the end of the story. The women went merely to embalm a dead body.

The two men walking to Emmaus were actually leaving Jerusalem to return to their homes and jobs.

The apostles hiding in the Upper Room were clearly unprepared for the risen Saviour's sudden presence among them.

It was he who had to prove the reality of his new life in the most matter-of-fact and conclusive way, by eating and drinking before their very eyes; and by forcing Thomas to touch his mortal wounds.

St. Paul is equally factual in persuading the Corinthians of the truth of the resurrection. He himself is so convinced that he bases on it his whole argument for the religion to which he has been converted. "If Christ has not risen then our preaching is groundless, and your faith, too is groundless. Worse still, we are convicted of giving false testimony about God."

Nobody, neither enemy nor friend, was in any doubt that Christ had claimed to be God. It was for that claim that he had been done to death, as a blasphemy against God and a deceiver of the people.

"Come down from that cross, if thou art the Son of God, and we will believe. He trusted in God; let God, if he favours him, succour him now." The challenge was accepted far more convincingly than it was put. It wasn't the living Christ who came down from the cross. He chose first to die as the Redeemer, even of those who mocked at his death.

EASTER: THE REALITY OF CHRIST'S RESURRECTION

The body of the Risen Christ was a real human body. Of that we can be certain, thanks to the Apostles, whose own doubts, quite forcibly expressed, gave our Lord the opportunity to reassure them, and us, with equal forthrightness.

Terrified that theirs might be the fate of their crucified Master, they had not only run away but had hidden in the Upper Room and locked the doors behind them. Then suddenly he was in their midst. No wonder they shrank back in fear, thinking they were "seeing things." They were just in the frame of mind for that. Jesus at once gave them the confidence they had so lacked. And as practical proof of how very human he was, the Divine Saviour asked them for food and they gave him fish which he ate as they stared at him bewildered with joy but at last convinced.

But the Apostle Thomas had missed all this and he wasn't going to be convinced till our Lord went all through the ritual of "seeing is believing" for him. Yet not for him alone. The Saviour was thinking of us, even more than Thomas.

Pope St. Gregory the Great pointed this out in commenting on that second appearance, eight days later.

> The divine clemency brought it about in a wonderful way that the doubting disciple, while touching the wounds in his master's flesh, should thereby heal the wounds of our unbelief.
>
> The unbelief of Thomas is more to our faith than the faith of the believing disciples. While he is brought back to faith by touching, our minds are set free from doubt and established in the faith.

EASTER: WE TOO WILL RISE

During Our Lord's "second life" of forty days, between his resurrection and ascension, his bodily senses were the same as before. He enjoyed the faculties of sight, hearing, taste, touch, smell, but none were subject to fatigue or pain. Nor did he suffer any physical need. When he asked his Apostles for food, it was simply to convince them of the reality of his body.

For the same purpose of convincing his Apostles of his victory over death, he kept the scars of his crucifixion, though for the rest of us, when our bodies rise to immortal glory, such marks of mortality will have disappeared.

Our Lord's risen body had two other powers. He could move from place to place with the speed of thought, which explains his various sudden comings and goings. And lastly his body had taken on a quality St. Thomas Aquinas calls "clarity," whereby the physical features reflect the shining glory of the soul enjoying the Vision of God. This will explain why, on several occasions, the disciples did not immediately recognise their Master in the "new look" of his glorified body.

The reality of the Saviour's resurrection is a warranty of ours. So too are its characteristics. St. Paul was quick to point out:

> "You may ask, how are the dead raised? In what kind of body? A senseless question! . . . The dead will rise immortal and we shall be changed. What is mortal shall be clothed with immortality . . . Then the sayings of Scripture will come true: 'Death is swallowed up; victory is won!' God be praised. He gives us the victory through our Lord Jesus Christ."

CHRIST'S GRAND DESIGN

Christ's Ascension took place on Mount Olivet. For forty days, Our Lord had met his Apostles many times, appearing suddenly and unexpectedly, his glorified body no longer restricted by time or distance, yet none the less real, as he kept proving to them by eating with them, and letting them touch him.

He spent those weeks not only reassuring their senses as to the reality of his conquest of death, but also recapping, so to speak, on all that he had previously taught them and which the terrifying events of his Passion and Crucifixion had left so confused in their minds.

Now came the last meeting, official and by appointment. He had ordered them back to Jerusalem to see him off home to his Father, his task accomplished. For them it was both an end and a beginning. They sensed instinctively the importance of the occasion and without hesitation "they fell down to worship." They had full faith in him now as their God as well as their Lord. And they awaited his final commission to them. "All authority in heaven and on earth has been given to me. You must go out all over the world and preach the Gospel, making disciples of all nations."

There was Christ's grand design for a truly Catholic and Universal Church, at this moment little more than the mustard seed he had planted in tiny Palestine, but in the course of time and to the end of time to embrace all peoples in the Mystical Body of Christ here on earth, in preparation for joining him forever in the happiness of Heaven.

ASCENSION: CHRIST ALWAYS WITH US

The Ascension, the final proof of Christ's divinity, ended his physical sojourn on earth, but he has remained with us, and will remain, as he promised, "always, even to the end of the world."

He is with us and in us, truly present in the Sacrament of his abiding love. He is also bound closely to us, and we to him, in his Church, of which he is the head and we the members, for the Church is the Mystical Body of Christ, the permanent continuation, till the end of time, of the Incarnation of Christ on earth.

All that lies at the heart of our Catholic Faith. One who did not share it and whose name is unknown has paid this moving tribute to the short life that changed the world:

He never did one of the things that accompany greatness. He had no credentials but himself.

While still a young man, the tide of popular opinion turned against him. His friends ran away. One of them denied him.

He was turned over to his enemies.

He went through the mockery of a trial. He was nailed to a cross between two thieves. His executioners gambled for the only piece of property he had on earth while he was dying — and that was his coat.

When he was dead he was taken down and laid in a borrowed grave through the pity of a friend.

Nineteen wide centuries have come and gone, and today he is the cornerstone of the human race and the keystone of the Kingdom of God.

When I say that all the armies that ever marched, and all the navies that ever were built, and all the parliaments that ever sat, and all the kings that ever reigned, have not affected the life of men as powerfully as that One Solitary Life — none will be found to disagree.

PENTECOST: THE WIND
AND THE FIRE

The manner of the Holy Spirit's coming at Pentecost has deep significance. There was "the sound of a strong wind blowing," and "what seemed to be tongues of fire parted and came to rest on each of them."

Wind and fire were apt outward signs for the inward grace conferred. The main property of both is energy and power, destructive and consuming when out of hand, yet who can say that of the wind and fire of Pentecost held within the hand of their divine maker?

Wind is also refreshing to the mind through the body. "Bracing brain and sinew, blow, thou wind of God." Fire not only consumes, it transforms and, in all human languages, the word is used as a figure of speech to describe the transformation brought about in the spirit of a man by the ardour of an ideal.

Can you see now why God the Holy Spirit chose the natural powers of wind and fire to signify the supernatural effect of his coming?

He certainly blew the cobwebs of lassitude and lack of understanding from the minds of the Apostles and replaced them with an energetic fiery zeal. This was at once evident in Peter's magnificent first sermon heard by a crowd of Jews on pilgrimage to Jerusalem from distant lands. It was a meaningful miracle.

The first Christians were Jews, but their mandate given them by Christ was to proclaim the good news of salvation to all nations, and here they were fulfilling it by the power of the Holy Spirit. The Church of Christ, on this her birthday, already showed herself to be truly Catholic.

55

PENTECOST: THE SPIRIT THAT MOVES

In the early days of evangelisation the Holy Spirit was so obviously with the Apostles and their helpers, overcoming the human and practical difficulties of communicating and sustaining the new-formed faith of the first converts by divine intervention promised by Christ himself.

The fulfilment of that promise was seen in the extraordinary change brought about in the minds and hearts of the Apostles themselves at Pentecost: "It has seemed good to the Holy Ghost and to us," is their confident cry. From now on they are conscious of the Divine Spirit working in and through them.

St. Paul tried to bring home to his converts a realisation of the presence of the Holy Spirit in each one of them when he said: "Don't you know that you are the temples of the Holy Ghost? That you have the Spirit of God dwelling within you?"

We need to be reminded of that Presence as much, and maybe more, than the first Christians did. It is often the obvious that we overlook and neglect. And what could be easier than to turn in silent prayer to the "Soul's delightsome guest?" In those teasing doubts about your faith, remember, "He is the Light of all that live." When the salt of devotion loses its savour, ask him then: "On our dryness pour thy dew."

In daily difficulties that so often sour our lives, he will help to "bend the stubborn heart and will, melt the frozen, warm the chill, guide the steps that go astray." All this he will do, fulfilling Christ's promise that "the Holy Spirit will be your friend."

PENTECOST: THE CALL

On Pentecost Sunday we commemorate the birthday of the Church, the Mystical Body of Christ, comprising all men and women who are redeemed by his Passion and Death. On this day our Lord fulfilled his promise to ask his Father to send down the Holy Spirit upon his Apostles and instructed them to "Go forth and teach all nations," and thereby established his Church of which we are a part.

We sometimes hear people say: "He is going into the Church," as if the Church merely consisted of those who are ordained to the Priesthood. That is not true. The laity are just as much a part of the Church of Christ as are bishops, priests, nuns and, indeed, the pope. While this has been true throughout the history of the Church, it was only at the recent Ecumenical Council that this truth was re-emphasised and the urgent need to bring the laity into the day-to-day administration of the Church was underlined. We have seen the Pope appoint notable laymen and women to sit on advisory committees. The Hierarchy are turning more and more to the laity for advice upon innumerable matters. No longer are layfolk merely souls to be saved, but an integral part of the Church, with an apostolic mission arising from the Sacraments of Baptism and Confirmation.

The Hierarchy has shown faith in the laity. Have you sufficient Faith to obey the call of Pentecost? Our forefathers had and they went in fear of their lives. They so loved Almighty God and our Blessed Lord in the Holy Mass that they were prepared to risk everything. The Faith has been handed down to us inviolate, by those who retained their Faith throughout penal times. They have handed down the Faith into our keeping. Are we going to turn away from our responsibilities? Of course not. We are going to face the facts, because we too love Almighty God, because we too have the Faith, because we too love our Lord in the Blessed Sacrament. So we too must show that when we are tested we are as staunch as were our ancestors, martyrs and confessors to the one true Church.

PENTECOST: OF ALL CONSOLERS BEST

"Unless a man be born again of water and the Holy Spirit, he cannot enter into the Kingdom of God," said our Divine Lord.

We have all had the blessing of rebirth in Baptism. At our Confirmation the Holy Spirit became "the sweet guest of the soul," bringing his sevenfold gift. Even should we drive him away by grievous sin, he returns at our first murmur of repentance in the confessional.

Are we to remain just passive in his presence? Having become "partakers of the Holy Spirit" (Hebr. 6:4), our responsibility to co-operate with such grandeur of grace is very great. It is a case of *noblesse oblige*. No mere avoidance of sin is sufficient for us, who are called to be "sharers in the Divine Nature." Understanding something of the part the Holy Spirit plays in our souls, we must make ourselves increasingly conscious of his presence and turn to him constantly in prayer.

There are many moments throughout our day when we, who live and work largely in an atmosphere of unbelief and indifference to all moral obligation, will need to call on our "soul's delightsome guest, of all consolers best" to strengthen our faith, to grant us the supreme gift of sorrow for sin, to renew our fervour and even to guide us in the manifold decisions, religious and otherwise, we have to make on our daily round.

> *Heal our wounds, our strength renew;*
> *On our dryness pour thy dew;*
> *Wash the stains of guilt away.*
> *Bend the stubborn heart and will;*
> *Melt the frozen, warm the chill;*
> *Guide the steps that go astray.*

TRINITY: EXPLORING
THE INFINITE

The Mystery of the Blessed Trinity demands a more complete submission of our minds to Divine Revelation than other tenets of our Faith. We can never fully understand the inner life of God, but we already know a great deal from what God-made-Man has told us. Our handicap is that we are groping towards the Infinite with finite minds, groping at what we can touch but never fully grasp.

The unity of love in the Trinity of Persons was set before us by the Son of God as the standard of perfection, always to be striven for, even if never attained, in the lives of his followers. "Holy Father, keep them true to thy name . . . that they may be one, as we are one. That they may be one in us, as thou, Father, art in me, and I in thee."

That love for each other which we speak of as Christian Charity is, in fact, a pale reflection of Divine Charity within the Godhead. We could, indeed, speak of Trinity Charity as the perfection of love that we are to aim at and Christian Charity as what we actually achieve.

The happiness of Mankind depends on whether God's Creatures, loved with an everlasting love, will respond to that love which is of the very stuff of God's nature, "the Love of God, poured out unto our hearts by the Holy Spirit, whom we have received."

TRINITY: THE MYSTERY
OF THE GODHEAD

The Three-in-One that is God must always remain a mystery in our minds. If we were able wholly to explain and understand God, it would mean that God didn't exist. That's not a mere paradox. When a nuclear scientist, or a biologist or an anatomist pulls apart, analyses and explains the atom or a plant or an animal, it means that the human brain is greater than the subjects with which it copes and the problem it overcomes. If we could do that with God, God would be someone less than ourselves or, in other words, not God.

When you and I think a thought, our thought has no existence outside our own minds. When the Eternal, Infinite Mind of God, thinks of himself, this thought is as eternal and infinite and personal as himself. He expresses himself utterly. That is why we speak of the Word of God and call this Child of God's Mind, the Son.

The Father sees himself in the Son. The Son sees himself in the Father. And the bond between them is love, as eternal, infinite and personal as themselves. This conscious response of love that proceeds from Father to Son, from Son to Father, is the Holy Spirit.

In isolation, our lives have no meaning whatsoever. We are brought into life by the love of our parents. Our lives blossom and bloom in the love of our parents, our family and our friends. And when we try and learn to love as God loves, our love widens to embrace a host of people around us, some easy, some difficult to love, but all essentially lovable, because all like ourselves, are the children of God and the objects of his love which is within the Blessed Trinity.

PROMISES ARE TO BE KEPT

A promise is a promise and must be kept at the time and in the manner undertaken. Yet how lightly we often treat our obligations. It was a cynic (Jonathan Swift) who said: "Promises, like pie-crusts, are made to be broken." Yet a broken promise is a double lie, first spoken and then enacted by default. Shakespeare says of the great Wolsey after his death:

> His promises were, as he then was, mighty,
> But his performance, as he is now, nothing.

It's often a weakness of self-centred, self-satisfied types that they make all sorts of promises to look big without any real intention of carrying them out if they consider the person promised "doesn't matter." What a monstrous thing to say of God's creatures and what an insult to God.

We often treat promises lightly when we find they're going to cause us an inconvenience we didn't foresee. Yet the inconvenience is generally far more serious to the person promised and to brush that aside is sheer selfishness.

What a blessed thing it is to be able to trust each other to keep our promises to help each other. As we say, it's a weight off our minds: and it makes for a warm feeling of friendship and mutual respect that is the hallmark of Christianity.

Faith and Trust in him were what Christ asked of his followers before all else. And in his turn, he, who is the Word of God, could — and can — always be relied on to keep his word:

> Who broke no promise, served no private end,
> Who gained no title and who lost no friend.

61

DEPENDING ON ONE ANOTHER

There's a good and bad side to division of labour and dependence on others. God has given all of us head and hands and most people like using both to have a shot at playing the handy-man, with the help of one of those "Do-it-yourself" books which are so popular. That's as it should be. You're fulfilling God's purpose by using the latent talent he has given you. Think of it that way next time you mend a fuse. If you don't, there's a danger in this kind of self-sufficiency; in fact, a double danger.

First, if we forget that the abilities we're so proud of are sheer gifts of God, we become self-centred, self-satisfied, and whenever we think too much of self, well, we think too much of ourselves.

The second danger of this self-reliance is that it is, to some extent, anti-social. We're much more likely to have a proper respect for others as persons, created by God with talents denied to us, once we realise how much we depend on others.

You probably enjoy your cup of tea with milk, fresh milk, but a lot has happened since it left the cow and a lot of people have worked hard to get it to you. So it is with the hundred-and-one goods and services that make up our daily lives. They're done by persons who rely on us in other ways, just as we rely on them. We depend on each other, and the confidence we all have that, by and large, this confidence wasn't misplaced, is the kingpin that enables our rather complicated lives to run so smoothly.

JUDGE NOT

Many of us are given to rash judgments. We sometimes speak about others or act towards them as if the Last Day were already over and gone. But when we examine our own conscience, we have to acknowledge that our ideas were prompted by some paltry prejudice. We did it because we happened to be in a bad mood. We did it because we are suspicious by nature, we are victims of that dismal disease of seeing evil everywhere.

The good names of scores of people lie in wreck and ruin about us, we have roused hatred and envy, broken friendships, started feuds and quarrels; but unheeding, we go our way, quite pleased with our superior insight and rectitude.

Thank God not many go thus far; they sin by rash judgment only in thought. They happily keep their thoughts to themselves. In such cases their sin is indeed less, yet it remains a sin after all. Even in the secrecy of our hearts we may not needlessly sit in judgment on the lives of others. God, who reads our thoughts, will call us to account for the pride, the envy, the heartlessness which underlie our rash, tacit condemnation of our neighbour. "A man judges others by himself." A good man does not rightly think evil of his brother; a bad man thinks others as bad as himself.

By imputing motives a man betrays his own soul. Let us banish from our souls any dark, uncharitable thoughts and force ourselves to think well of others whenever possible. If, on examining our conscience we find that we have harboured unfounded suspicions, let us drive them away for Christ's sake. He has shown us mercy beyond our deserts; let our thoughts be merciful even as his.

SELF-COMPLACENCY

Blessed are the peace-makers! It's a blessing we'd all like to earn. But the would-be peace-maker must first be at peace with himself. A worried, warring mind cannot radiate serenity around it. Personal peace must precede collective peace.

Yet there is such a thing as false personal peace, a sort of self-complacency — everything that I say and do is right — a self-satisfaction that can be a source of intense irritation to others, in fact, a disturber of the peace.

The greatest gift God has given us, after life itself, is our individuality. We're not machine-made types, mass-produced. But the very fact that we're individuals, all a bit different from each other, means that we tend to be preoccupied with self, to be self-centred.

Even in the little circle of those we love, our family and friends, there's an urge to be in the centre of the picture. Yet someone has said that to do that is to make friendship impossible. Maybe that's an exaggeration, but you can see what he means. Friendship demands complete equality, admiration and love that are mutual, a sharing of confidence and trust.

To insist on always being Number One is an irritant that corrodes the foundation of friendship. It soon replaces respect with something akin to contempt. A conversation with too many "I"s in it ends with someone's nose being put out of joint!

Extreme egoism runs dangerously close to the blasphemy of self-worship and is, thank God, rare, but all of us tend to think too much of ourselves — especially, I'm afraid, we men.

If we could see ourselves as others see us, we just wouldn't believe it! Yes, I know that when our qualities are under discussion we put on a fine air of self-depreciation, but woe betide anyone who takes us at our word. He'll soon come under the lash of our tongue — when his back is turned.

This false modesty of ours is all the more nauseating because it bears no relation to the truth. First we pretend to be less capable than in fact we are; which is lie number one. Then we claim for ourselves the credit for such abilities as we have; which is lie number two. Listen to St. Paul on the subject: "What powers have you, that did not come to you by gift? And if they came to you by gift, why do you boast of them, as if there were no gift in question?"

The fact is, we possess nothing that isn't a loan-on-trust from God. Therefore any credit or praise for these gifts must necessarily go not to me but to God.

So I've nothing to be proud or conceited about, except that God favours me more than I can ever deserve. Humility demands that I acknowledge the truth, seeing things as they are. And this truth-seeing humility also requires that I admit my good qualities; to deny or belittle them is an insult to God who gave them to me. But I must go a step further and admit that, even though I'm the trustee of God's gifts, I cannot even begin to use them well without his help, for it is only "by the grace of God I am what I am." All I can do is to thank God, as St. Paul did, that "His grace in me hath not been void."

THE VALUE OF SIMPLICITY

As individuals, in regard to ourselves, our friends and neighbours, and even to God, we tend to create problems and difficulties that don't exist outside our imagination. We're not simple enough. Indeed, we've perverted the meaning of the word. Simple-minded means to us "foolish, ignorant, inexperienced, half-witted." I'm not making that up. I got it from a dictionary.

In fact, "simple-minded" should mean "single-minded," going straight to the truth. Simplicity is frankness mixed with a certain shrewdness. The sort of thing you get in little children who are quite artless, direct and uncomplicated. It's we so-called intelligent adults who have forgotten how to be simple. Having grown out of the fresh simplicity of our childhood, we take up a sophisticated attitude towards life and manufacture problems which don't exist.

We're rarely content with our little lot in life. We plot and plan and promise to do something someday really worth doing. If only we'd been born lucky like so-and-so. If only we'd had a better start in life. If only — it's always that "if only." And the fact that we haven't got the advantages we covet tempts us to turn sour with envy of those who have them. We may even work up a grudge against God. We know in theory that there must be inequalities in life; that there are many worse off than ourselves. But if only *we* — there we go again!

If only we would accept God's will, which is to make the best of what He has given us. More than that, we need to see with child-like directness that what the world calls little is great in God's eyes, if the little is all he wants of us and we do it well.

CRITICISM

The word "critic" comes from the Greek, meaning to judge or assess, to form a balanced judgment. It is typical of the way we often twist words away from their basic sense when the dictionary says "critical" means censorious or fault-finding. Far better is Matthew Arnold's definition of criticism as "a disinterested endeavour to learn and propagate the best."

It's all too easy to pick out the faults of others and yet it's a fruitless pastime that boomerangs back on ourselves, because when we're dealing with people, fault-finding never brings out the best in them. It merely tends to blind us to that best, while at the same time it makes the other person uncertain of himself and either unable or unwilling to give of his best.

Out of sheer self-interest, though also from the higher motive of Christian charity or justice, we should always look for the finest qualities in others and try to foster them. You'll be the better able to do this, if you ask yourself these questions and can answer them right.

Do you rejoice at the success of others?
Do you give credit where it's due?
Are you a good listener?
Do you encourage others to offer ideas?
Do you seek advice of those more expert than yourself?
Do you treat others as you wish to be treated yourself?

BEWARE OF GOSSIP

"Words, words, words," sang the heroine of "My Fair Lady." Remember? Whether spoken or written, words are both a privilege and a responsibility. They're the means God has given us of communicating to each other the thoughts that are in our minds.

Beware of garrulous gossip. It's a waste of precious time to use a dozen words when one will do. Once you start speaking of others, you'll almost certainly exaggerate, which is a kind of lying, and you may lapse into uncharitableness. And if you're tempted to speak of yourself, remember Chesterton's definition of a bore as one who talks about himself when you want to talk about yourself.

We're responsible even more for words we write than for those we speak. A passing remark may soon be forgotten. The written word remains as evidence for or against you. Re-read your letters before you post them and don't hesitate to re-write or even tear them up, if you have the slightest doubt of their being hurtful rather than helpful.

Because of its wider and anonymous impact, the printed word is the greatest responsibility of all. No writer had a deeper sense of this than that master of words, grave and gay, witty and profound, the late Monsignor Ronald Knox. Here is part of a prayer found among his unpublished papers at his death:

My God, what I have written does not belong to me. If I have written the truth, then it is "God's truth." It would be true if every mind denied it, or if there were no human minds in existence to recognise it . . . So I would ask that among all the millions of souls you cherish, some few, upon the occasion of reading it, may learn to understand you a little, and to love you more.

LIVING FOR OTHERS

Are you an introvert or an extrovert? What do the words mean? Literally, a turning *in* on oneself, a preoccupation with one's ego, or a turning *out* from oneself towards others.

The introvert tends towards being so absorbed in the little world of his inner conflicts and dissatisfied yearnings that he is in danger of acute melancholia and pessimism. All of which makes him a bad mixer.

The extrovert, on the other hand, is hail-fellow-well-met, a back-slapper, often a non-stop talker, and generally reckoned good company — for a time, anyway. He is the supreme optimist, sometimes a little shallow. His saving quality is that he's nearly always ready to do anybody a good turn, whereas the introvert is so wrapped up in himself that he doesn't know how to, and is often so soured with life that he doesn't want to.

While avoiding the extremes of introversion and extroversion we should, as Christians, practise a little of both. We are all bound to be, if not introverts, at least introspective to the extent of examining our consciences, to look into the depths of our souls, to see whether our innermost self is attuned to God and at harmony with outward actions. That self-examination must be done in all humility, making us realise our faults and our need of God's grace to overcome them. This introspection must, in its turn, take us outside ourselves to fulfil our manifold duties to others.

The spiritual life is a love affair between my soul and God, but because God loves all his children, our love for him cannot be separated from practical love-in-action towards each other. To live not for ourselves but for others is the true fulfilment of self.

OTHERS' FAULTS ARE OURS

"There's so much good in the worst of us." You know the rest of the jingle, but just think over that first line.

You'll be the better able to do this, if you ask yourself these questions and can answer them aright:

Do you encourage others to offer ideas?

Do you seek the advice of those more expert than yourself?

Do you invite constructive criticism?

Do you frankly admit your mistakes and take the blame for them?

Do you delegate to others their share of responsibility or do you let the "Cause," whatever it is, suffer by making it a one-man operation?

Do you allow individuals the freedom they need and deserve to do their job well?

Do you encourage the legitimate self-interest that everyone needs in his work?

Do you recognise the particular contribution your associates or helpers make?

Do you treat others as you wish to be treated yourself?

Finally, dwell on these words of wisdom. "We see other men's mistakes, other men see ours, so necessary is mutual candour and charity, because he who forgiveth today may have need to be forgiven tomorrow."

HYPOCRISY

Do you know what the word Hypocrite meant originally? It's the Greek for actor, someone who plays a part. But don't all of us do that — and quite often? I don't mean within the four walls of a theatre, but on the wider stage called Life. What was it Shakespeare wrote? "All the world's a stage. And all the men and women merely players. They have their exits and their entrances. And one man in his time plays many parts."

You and I are playing a part and, to that extent, playing the hypocrite, whenever we listen politely to a crashing bore; whenever we control our tempers or our tongues; whenever, if you like, we take Christ at his word, and try to see him in our weaker brethren. But there's virtue in putting on that kind of act. That's not what Christ condemned.

The kind of hypocrisy that sickened Christ, and drew from him such searing contempt and denunciation is when we set ourselves up as models of virtue and glory in it, taking all the credit to ourselves, boasting even to God of our goodness, as the Pharisees did.

By contrast, there was the despised publican; conscious only of his shortcomings, he prayed: "God, be merciful to me. I am a sinner." That is the kind of prayer that wins God's favour. And the judgment Christ passed on those two is the same he will pass on us. Everyone who exalts himself will be humbled, and the man who humbles himself will be exalted.

Lord Jesus, make me so utterly sincere in all I say and do, that others may see in me a reflection of you. Never let my bad example be a cause of scandal to others, that because of me they reject you.

THE SECRET OF HAPPINESS

What is the secret of happiness? I suppose there are as many answers as seekers after happiness, and that means all of us. Probably no two of us will agree on what we seek, save it is a will-o'-the wisp, slipping from our grasp at the very moment we think we've found it.

A dear friend of mine has wise words to say on the subject in his autobiography, *Life's Adventure*.

It is the people with a strong and simple faith who, I believe, have the best chance of happiness. It gives them a sense of proportion regarding the things that matter and don't matter: a better sense of values. Ordinary simple men and women are sustained by a belief in divine goodness and pity and love.

Now, as the perfect happiness for which our Creator has destined us is to love him and be loved by him for all eternity, the secret of happiness in this world is to begin that exchange of love, to be on loving terms with God, here and now. That, as our Lord said, is the first and greatest commandment. He added that the second is like to it, namely, to love one's neighbour as oneself.

It follows, surely, that mutual love between us and our fellow men is part of the secret of happiness. As love is not a taking but a giving, it means that the essence of happiness, both here and hereafter, lies not, as so many think, in self-satisfaction, which is mere pleasure, but in that self-giving which is love.

THE INNER YEARNING

We can't help yearning for happiness; it's elusive, but always beckoning. There are times when we think we have it in our grasp at last, but never for long. Soon it slips away and off we go on our search again, ever hopeful. That's life as it is and as God wants it. He wants us to keep striving hopefully for happiness. He teases us at times with snatches of happiness, but he doesn't let them last for long, because he hasn't put us into this world for complete, unending happiness.

He's deliberately implanted in us a yearning that can never in fact be fully satisfied in this life by anything or anyone that may for the moment please mind or body. Yet he wants us to enjoy all the good things he's given us in this life — to eye and ear, taste and smell. He wants us, still more, to savour the deeper spiritual satisfaction of the mind, made in his image.

But while we enjoy all he offers us in this life, he wants us to see, as indeed we must if we think at all, that they're not wholly satisfying. He's made us all Oliver Twists, always asking for more, and the more is God.

St. Augustine suddenly saw this quite clearly, when after tasting every pleasure of body and mind that life could offer him, still dissatisfied, he cried out to God: "Thou has made us for thyself and our heart is restless till it find rest in thee."

RESTLESS HEARTS

Our capacity for knowing and loving isn't just confined to things and people around us. Our mind is capable of knowing its own Maker, God, and until it is used for that, until it is occupied to its fullest capacity, it isn't fulfilling its highest purpose, and isn't completely happy.

If you shut your eyes to God's Providence for the world in general and you in particular, you're like a watch without hands. It ticks over quite happily, but it doesn't fulfil the purpose for which it's made. Neither do you, unless you see your life as God-given and God-destined.

If you bring God into your life you'll be living in a much fuller way than you do now; and therefore you'll have a greater happiness and contentment than you have now, and moreover, you can still take life as it comes. Yet not as a chancy, meaningless succession of days but as a God-given and God-planned succession of days.

How often he's going to repeat his gift of days to you and me is his own affair, not ours. All God wants from you and me is to live this present day well. So let us pray with the Psalmist: "Teach us to count every passing day, till our hearts find wisdom."

OUR GOD-GIVEN PURPOSE

Most of us look on the bright side and take life as it comes and, if at times it comes rough — well, we quickly adapt ourselves to circumstances and make the best of them. As the Cockney girl said: "Life ain't all you want but it's all you 'ave, so 'ave it. Stick a geranium in yer 'at and be 'appy.'

Now that's all very fine, as far as it goes, but it doesn't go far enough. It doesn't go far enough if we mean by it that this life of ours is just a chance affair that's happened to us. It's the only thing I'm certain of, so I'll make the best of it, extract all the juice I can out of the orange and then throw the peel away. "Eat, drink and be merry for tomorrow we die." That sort of attitude to life is common enough but it's wrong on two counts.

First, it doesn't allow God any say in this life and secondly, it rules out any future life or at any rate says we don't really know, so why get into a flap about it? If there is a hereafter, we'll just take a chance. There's that word "chance" again. We're looking on life as a game of chance, playing the Football Pools. It's not. It's a game of skill.

We're persons of intelligence and that mind of ours hasn't just come into existence by chance. The cogs and springs of your watch haven't fallen together by chance, have they?

God, the maker of the human mind, has so arranged its mechanism that its purpose is to know and to love. If it doesn't do that, it fails in its purpose. It's useless. But when the human mind does work to know and love, it fulfils its purpose and, because it belongs to a person, its knowing and loving satisfy that person. In other words, to know and to love is to be happy.

WHAT IS THIS GOD?

"Late have I loved thee." In these words, St. Augustine chiselled a throbbing phrase of regret for a wasted past, of buoyant hope in the future. A cry that surely finds an echo in the heart of every one of us.

St. Augustine's amazing mind, with its overpowering passion for intellectual truth, has told the story of his conversion in what is Literature's first great personal book; making frank avowal of his sins with all the humility of a great soul. He had wandered far from God seeking the solace of earthly joys of mind and body. He tells of his puzzled search in phrases to be echoed 1,500 years later in *The Hound of Heaven,* by Francis Thompson.

What is this God? I asked the earth and it answered, "I am not he," and all things that are in the earth made the same confession. I asked the sea and the deeps and the creeping things, and they answered, "We are not your God, seek higher." I asked the heavens, the sun, the moon, the stars, and they answered, "Neither are we God whom you seek." And I said to all the things that throng about the gateways of the senses, "Tell me something of him." And they cried out in a great voice, "He made us." My question was my gazing upon them, and their answer was their beauty . . . I asked the whole frame of the universe about my God and it answered me, "I am not he, but he made me."

MAN, THE VOICE OF NATURE

Lordship over Nature is God's special charge to Man which, with present day advances in technology and medical science, is a very grave responsibility. He's given to Man a mind created in his own likeness. The lesser orders of Nature, the plants and animals, God has created without that inner self-guidance we call the intellect. God has, of course, placed within them laws of life and growth, but to give of their best they need guidance and control from outside themselves. God could have undertaken that himself, by direct divine intervention, but he chose instead to delegate some of his powers to Man.

Man is master of the world, but only as God's agent. His mastery, great though it is, is itself God's gift, and the objects of that mastery are God's creatures lent to Man for his use and enjoyment.

God has done this for a two-fold purpose — that Man may fulfil his two-fold life — the life of the body and the life of the spirit. The rich store-house of Nature is at man's disposal to nourish the needs of his body — to provide him with food and drink, clothing and shelter. But in using God's gifts, Man is also meant to use his mind to see whence and why they are at his disposal; to see in them evidence of God's loving kindness and to acknowledge it.

Man has a double duty to praise and thank God for his goodness; for himself and for the rest of creation, which cannot speak for itself. Plants, flowers, animals give glory to God by being what they are; creatures of usefulness, strength and beauty.

Yet none of them knows that they are such or why. But Man does. Unknowingly, they give their Maker glory. They cannot give thanks. Man alone can do that. He is the Voice of Nature.

OUR LASTING VALUE

"A riddle wrapped in a mystery, enclosed in an enigma." Is that what you think life is? An insoluble puzzle? A meaningless muddle of pleasures and pains — pleasures that tease only to deceive; pains that never lie, for they warn us of the approach of death, inexorable, unavoidable? If you think that, think again! For the very fact that you're able to think means this life isn't the meaningless muddle it sometimes seems on the surface.

We know, if we think for a moment, that everything we do is done for a purpose; it may be good, like doing an act of kindness; it may be bad, like stealing; it may be trivial, like scratching your ear. But we have a reason for doing all these things. And don't you think God has a reason, a purpose, for everything that he's done?

It's that grand design that we call Providence, by which he created and goes on creating and running this world of ours as a going concern. But God isn't just concerned with the world as a whole any more than the clock-maker is only concerned with the finished product that appears in the shop window.

God, like the clock-maker, has a particular purpose for everything that goes to make up his world, and that means you and me. You, and that mind and heart of yours which we call the soul, are capable, however unimportant a person you may be, of great thoughts and great love. They're, in a sense, your creation. In other words, you're a little bit like God, as the Bible says. You're not just a passing whim and fancy of God's. You're made to last, and last forever.

EDUCATION FOR HEAVEN

"Why do we educate except to prepare for this world?" It was Cardinal Newman who put that question and the answer seems hardly what you'd expect from him. It has a utilitarian ring about it that is more typical of the present day outlook that tends more and more to regard education simply as the acquiring of specialised knowledge, especially in the field of science, as training for a job and not the discipline of the mind as such.

Cardinal Newman, of course, never held so narrow a view, yet he said that "If a liberal education be good, it must necessarily be useful too." Useful for the life of this world but, as he was careful to add: "This world is in all its circumstances a trial for the next."

Once you accept Man's spiritual nature and his ultimate destiny as a life of unending happiness with God, fulfilment of all our seeking after beauty, truth and goodness, then all education, all our acquiring of knowledge is beamed to that divine wavelength.

Eric Gill made the same point: "No longer can we think merely of getting on in the commercial and materialistic sense. We must now think of getting on in the sense of getting heavenwards." We must learn to get on in the world; not as an end in itself, but as a means of getting heavenwards.

All of which was summed up by the head teacher of a famous Catholic public school who, when asked at a Headmasters' Conference to state the aim and objective of the education given at his school, and for what it set out to prepare its pupils, simply said: "Death."

AN INFORMED CONSCIENCE

"Conscience doth make cowards of us all," says Hamlet. But conscience, fully informed and firmly followed, can make heroes of us all.

One of the most vexing problems of our day is the proper relationship between conscience and authority. Conscience means our awareness that, in this life of ours, in our relationship to our fellow men and to God, some things are good, some are bad, some are false, some are true. But which are which? Would you like to decide, in every case, for yourself alone? Or wouldn't you admit in all honesty, that you might be tempted to a bit of wishful thinking? That you might be inclined to choose as right or wrong, as true or false, what you wanted to be so?

Personal, subjective choice will always be open to doubt, unless checked by an objective norm, outside of oneself. That's the whole difference between the Catholic and the Protestant ethos. The latter relies on private judgment. The Catholic looks to an authority outside of himself to tell him what is right or wrong, true or false.

Yet the stress, since Vatican II, is all on personal choice, with Authority (pope, bishops, pastors) all too often, staying silent. Call this, if you like, as the Church does, a tribute to, and recognition of the dignity of the human person. But we mustn't forget that we belong to a fallen race. The individual needs to be guided by authority, for as Newman wrote:

> Conscience does not repose on itself, but vaguely reaches forward to something beyond self, and dimly discerns a sanction higher than self for its decisions. Unaided conscience is unable to arrest fierce wilful human nature . . . Let us beware of trifling with conscience.

COPING WITH TEMPTATION

St. James explains the process of passing from temptation to sin quite clearly.

> Each person is tempted when he is lured and enticed by his own desire. Then desire when it has conceived gives birth to sin, and sin when it is full-grown brings forth death.

There you see the two operations are quite distinct. First the enticement, which is temptation and not a sin. And then the yielding, the giving way, which is. Temptations of various kinds are part and parcel of life. Sometimes they seem purely mental or spiritual temptation — like *pride*, which is the root of all sin, or like the harsh thoughts we often have towards each other, or the doubts that torment us about God and his goodness.

That sort of thing appears at first sight to be the concern of the soul alone. But it's not true. We are creatures made up of both soul and body, which can't be separated save by death. So all our temptations spring from something that happens to us outside ourselves, even though it's the soul that has to face the burden of resistance.

It's because temptations are so many and so strong that we sometimes feel that the scales are weighted against us in our struggle for self-control. That feeling is itself a temptation — a temptation to forget that God is ready to help us at all times. The battle of life isn't a lonely struggle watched by an aloof and distant God: "When thou thinkest I am far from thee, I am often nearest to thee." God and his grace are there for the asking all the time. And because temptation will come whether we like it or not, our Lord told us to pray humbly and trustingly for God's guidance throughout our temptations and for his help not to yield to them:

> Even though I walk through the valley of the shadow of death, I fear no evil, for thou art with me. Thy rod and thy staff comfort me.

HOLINESS IS WHOLENESS

Holiness is something that many of us find frightening, especially when we are told that it is a necessary condition for getting to Heaven. The heroism of the saints doesn't help much. How can we, with all our limitations, ever hope to reach such heights? Pious people are sometimes more off-putting than the saints. But don't let us fall into the trap of invidious comparisons. Let's try and see what holiness really means. The word itself, first of all.

Holy has the same basic meaning as "whole." Just as sanctity is the same as "sane." In other words, we're well on the way to becoming holy, when we see the wholeness of life's purpose, our complete dependence on God, and order our own lives accordingly. That was, and is, the sanity of the saints; they see things straight, with the right sense of values, God's standards, and try to live up to them.

St. Thérèse of Lisieux hit the nail on the head when she wrote:

Holiness is not in one exercise or another, it consists in a disposition of the heart, which renders us humble and little in the hands of God, conscious of our weakness but confident, even daringly confident, in his fatherly goodness.

That puts holiness in a different light, doesn't it? After all, it should be obvious that there is no such person as a ready-made saint. We're all sinners trying to become a little less sinful so as to get nearer to God. That's the way we'll become holy, without even knowing it, for, as Robert Louis Stevenson once said: "The saints are the sinners who keep on trying."

OUR DEPENDENCE ON GOD

God wants you for keeps. His love brought you into life; his love keeps you alive, and his love promises you fullness of life such as you can't even imagine here. That's God's final purpose in making you, but he has another one, just for the few years of your life on earth. That purpose is to try you out, or rather, God wants to see how *you* try out that extraordinary power he's given you, that makes you a creature in his own image. In other words, the spiritual part of you, your soul, your mind, your will.

Firm faith in God lies at the very heart of life's meaning. And by faith, I don't mean a mere intellectual acceptance of the existence of a Supreme Being. Faith is all that but so much more. God is a person, just as you are, and faith in a person means trust in a person.

God isn't just someone to believe in, but to trust in, wholly, with complete confidence. And there's your virtue of Hope — arising out of faith in God and merging into Love of God. Faith, Hope and Love, these three, but the greatest of these is Love.

If God is all we firmly believe him to be, then we've everything to hope for — and that is that God loves us here and now with all our faults, and will be going on loving us forever, if only we'll trust him and let him have his way with us.

INCREASE OUR FAITH

"As you have faith in God, have faith in me," said Jesus Christ. There aren't many downright atheists in the world, thank God. But there are a lot of people about who think that there may be a God but he's so far removed from our way of life that we can't know a thing about him. How can we, unless we've someone to tell us, and tell us convincingly?

On the face of it, people who think that may have got something. St. Paul saw the difficulty and gave the answer: "How are they to call upon him, until they have learned to believe in him? And how are they to believe in him, without a preacher to listen to? Faith comes from hearing, and hearing, through Christ's Word."

As Christ himself explained: "No man has ever gone up into heaven. But there is one who has come down from heaven, the Son of Man who dwells in heaven." There were Christ's credentials. He belonged to both heaven and earth. And so Nicodemus exclaimed: "Master, we know that thou hast come from God to teach us."

It was faith that Christ kept asking for all the time. The answer that probably pleased him most was the one that expresses trustful confidence in him as a teacher, and a humble diffidence in ourselves as learners. This answer is also a prayer. Make it yours: "Lord, I do believe. Help thou my unbelief."

FAITH MEANS TRUST

The object of faith is truth, either abstract or factual, but it comes about through contact between persons; the one stating the fact, the other accepting his statement as true. Faith, therefore, has a vital and vitalising element of trust.

Between ourselves, when we sense an air of scepticism or doubt about something that we've said that we know is true, we at once react sadly, pleadingly, to the lack of trust implied: "But won't you take my word for it?"

Our Lord reacted in the same way, time and time again. "Why are ye fearful, ye of little faith?" He didn't demonstrate the truths he taught by logical argument, forcing our minds to assent. He stated a truth, and he asks us to accept his word for it.

Where faith is involved, it will be weak or strong in proportion to the trust and confidence we have in each other. The same test applies to divine or religious faith, but with this difference, that, whereas we can be led astray by each other, either deliberately or unintentionally, that can never happen with God who can neither deceive nor be deceived.

The mind must accept God's truth. However little of it we grasp is beside the point. The fact that he has spoken should be enough, for that is faith. And if it isn't enough, then the fault lies with us. Not in the mind but in the heart. It's not a question of "I cannot," but "I will not." The will to believe is lacking and that means a lack of trust and of love.

The answer is in the prayer that we cannot repeat too often: "Lord I do believe. Help thou my unbelief."

FAITH IS A GIFT

Faith and trust in Christ are all or nothing. There are those who seek a half-way house — to approach God through Christ, but not in and with Christ. For many, he is merely the perfect Man, the one in whom Divinity shines brightest.

He who, echoing the prophet Ezekiel, loved to call himself the Son of Man (and aren't we all?), was also the Son of God (and aren't we all?); but he was unique: Son of Man, Son of God, but before all and above all, God the Son, the Eternal Word, second Person of the Blessed Trinity, who, in the fullness of time, became incarnate ("and the Word was made flesh and dwelt among us"). The Man Jesus is Christ, who is God.

That is "the true image of Christ," which his vicar on earth, the Holy Father, asks us to accept. Pope Paul VI said:

Faith is not the result of an arbitrary or merely a naturalistic interpretation of the word of God. It is not the expression of the religious sense drawn, without legitimate guidance, from the opinion of many men who say they believe in God. Much less is it assent to the philosophical or sociological views current at a particular fleeting moment.

Faith is adherence with our entire spiritual being to the message of salvation communicated to us by revelation at once luminous and obscure.

Faith is not only search; above all, it is certitude. It is more than the result of human enquiry: it is a mysterious gift which demands docility and responsiveness for the wonderful dialogue that God conducts with us, if we are attentive and trustful.

THE MEANING OF HOPE

Hope is a favourite of mine. Squeezed between Faith and Charity, she seems like the Cinderella of the great Virtues. If that's so, the Cinderella Hope has two Ugly Sisters — Despair and Presumption.

Presumption is a brazen hussy who masquerades as Hope's lowly relative, but is in fact a false and seductive deceiver. Hope is both humble and confident, knowing she must play the part to earn her due reward, whereas Presumption takes reward for granted, arrogantly assuming it will come without effort.

Presumption is subtly deceptive because it puts on a pretence of being Hope at its highest. The presumptuous person professes to have such tremendous faith and confidence in God's merciful goodness that, no matter what he does or doesn't do, all will come right in the end. In Dickens's day, the presumptuous type was called Mr. Micawber. Nowadays it's the man who goes round saying airily: "I'm all right, Jack."

Maybe we're all a little bit guilty of presumption, because God is so infinitely patient with us. Anyway, too much hope isn't nearly as bad as none at all. But whereas Presumption is an airy expectation of getting something for nothing, Hope presupposes some effort on our part.

Hope is in a sense a two-way traffic between us and God. Our hopes in him are dependent on the fulfilment of his hope in us — that we will do our best to achieve the purpose for which he made us, which is to know, love and serve him in this life, so that he and we will be happy together forever in the next.

HOPE, THE ENEMY OF DESPAIR

All too many people sink deep into the Slough of Despond, feeling they've been more sinned against than sinning, blaming the unfair way they've been treated by life which they equate (quite rightly, in one sense) with God, the giver of life. So they turn against God for the sins of men. Life for them has been full of betrayers, full of pie-crust promises made only to be broken. If God lets that happen to ordinary decent people, then he can't be trusted.

Now that sort of thinking, so easy to slip into when you're badly depressed, can lead to sheer despair, and despair means that one ceases to believe, not necessarily in God's existence, but in God's goodness. So one gives up hope, and a man without hope has nothing to live for. Having lost the friendship of his fellows, he loses confidence in himself — and in his Maker.

Let each of us in our small way, by the example of our own loving trust in one another as well as in God, try to get over to those around us whose lives are bedevilled by despair (and despair is the Devil's supreme aim) that the answer to Mankind's malaise is a return to the love of God through faith and hope. Without hope man can never achieve his true destiny which is love of God through faith.

As despair brings the frustration of unhappiness to man, so hope brings happiness to the heart of man, a trusting faith that sees in life's darkest clouds, in the words of the poet, only the shade of God's hand "outstretched caressingly."

THE REWARD OF TRUST

Granted that life is full of stresses, strains and anxieties concerning our economic, social, family problems and on top of them all, the general permissiveness in faith as well as in morals, the fact is that we tend to worry far more over matters we can't control than those we can.

We get worked up over the latest crisis (a much overworked word these days, both in Church and State), yet we hardly give a second thought to a meanness or unkindness done to our neighbour, i.e. to Christ. We worry about what this world is coming to, instead of where we're going to — which is much more important.

There's only one way to overcome the pessimism and gloom so prevalent among us, both as Catholics and as citizens, and that is to renew our own personal faith and trust in God. This is God's world and you and I are the People of God. God's providence rules the world, and when all is said and done by men who, wielding immense power, seek to shape events to their own ends (falling for the first temptation named in Genesis "to be as gods"), in the end it is God's will that must prevail.

Have firm faith in that, especially when it's so hard to see and believe. The reward of trusting God is peace with God. Even in life's darkest moments, with all its harassments, its disappointments, its disillusions, if you cling on to hope, with utter confidence, you'll enjoy a tranquillity of mind, at peace with itself because at peace with God.

"My God, I have firm faith in your power: and trust always in your mercy."

OUR CARING GOD

The evil that overlays man's history, like an angry weal, has given us all a complex of fear — fear of what Léon Bloy called "the terrible absence of God." A silly thing to say! Of course God's there, but does he care?

How can he care when he allows all the devil's brew of disease, disaster and destruction to darken our lives? Can God care when he lets nature run riot, as in these terrible earthquakes that we hear about, and kill folk who can't take care of themselves?

That's the mentality rampant in the world today, isn't it? Suspicion, distrust, pessimism on all sides are dealing a death-blow to trust and confidence that we should have in God and in each other. In time of doubt, discouragement and distress, which are partly spiritual, partly emotional, we must try to put a brake on our emotions and argue ourselves back to unshakeable first principles.

What are they? First, God is a loving Father whose Providence guides the destiny of his children. In other words, it is love that makes the world go round. If we're tempted to think otherwise, it is because we have forgotten that we are the children of God. A little child never dreams that father or mother will fail it in need. Nor will they. I once asked a father and mother of a large family if they had any favourites. They said, "Yes, the one who happens to be ill." God's love is no different in kind, but only infinitely greater in degree.

GOD'S LOVING MERCY

Our Lord's main concern in the Gospels is for the moral and spiritual outcast. "Thy sins are forgiven thee. Go in peace." "Neither will I condemn thee; go and sin no more." The Father's joy at the return of the sinner is the theme of our Lord's most vivid parables: the Good Shepherd and the wandering sheep ("Rejoice with me, for I have found my sheep that was lost"), and the Prodigal Son, whose father, moved with compassion, ran towards him and kissed him.

God's merciful love is the recurring burden of the Gospel message. But does it give us a one-sided view of God? We know how stern Christ could be with malice of the mind, the hypocritical and unrepentant. We know God is a just God. In clinging to his mercy, which we so need, are we apt to ignore his justice, which we have good cause to shun?

In God there can be no contradiction. His mercy and his justice cannot clash; moreover, true justice isn't merely stern. In assessing guilt, it should take into account good intentions and circumstances that lessen responsibility. Such things a human judge may never know, but nothing escapes the all-seeing eye of God, and therefore it is true to say that God is merciful precisely because he is perfectly just.

If you're still afraid of life and waver in your trust in God your Father, remember that fear is a bad counsellor and gets you nowhere. But firm hope is all-powerful to touch and win over the heart of God.

GOD'S MERCIFUL LOVE

Love is a mystery that you can't explain. It's the driving force at the very heart of Life — and you can't explain that either. We just know that both exist, Life and Love, and that neither has true meaning without the other. But as both exist in us, who are created by God, we know that both exist in him first. God is Life, God is Love. He has imparted to us, whom he has made in his own image and likeness, a yearning that is first in him.

All creation is an act of love, so we ourselves are creatures of God's love. In creating us God has endowed us also with the power of loving and to give that love true meaning he has enabled us to say "Yes" or "No" to his love.

The fall from grace of the first man and woman was a refusal to love God. Just as the sin of every one of their descendants, down to our own selves, is a refusal to love. Such refusal, as we well know, is all too frequent, for we are weak and wayward, but happily it is rarely, if ever, final.

God's love for us is a merciful love and his grace is always at us, nudging, coaxing us to begin again to love him for his own sake, and to show our love for him by loving one another because he wills it. This is the least we can do. It is the best we can do, and all we need do, for "he who loves his neighbour has fulfilled the law."

TRUE LOVE IS MUTUAL

The course of true love, said Shakespeare, never did run smooth. Less poetic, but just as true: the path of true love should not be a one-way street. Love, to be a complete and perfect thing, must be mutual. Friend and friend, husband and wife, parents and children — the bond of love must run both ways, binding both.

God has made us that way — like himself. God, as in all else, is the supreme example of perfect love.

The love of God for us is that of a loving father, because he is so good and generous in his gifts to us, his children. Now if that love is to be complete, it needs response on our part. If that is lacking, the fault is ours. God loves us as a father, acts towards us as a father. It's up to us to love him as his children, to act towards him as his children.

In the order of nature we necessarily grow up, mature, and become independent of our parents, leading our own lives; but in the order of grace, in relation to God our Father, we must never grow up, we must never try to live our lives independent of him.

Our Lord drives home the lesson in a most striking incident recounted by three of the Gospel-writers. His Apostles grouped round him, he took a little child in his arms and said: "Believe me, unless you be converted and become like little children, you shall not enter into the Kingdom of Heaven."

In our approach to God our Father, we must strive to preserve in mind, heart and behaviour, the essential spirit of childhood which is a loving trust and confidence. It sounds simple enough, and so it is, simple, but it's the very opposite of easy.

THE LAW OF LOVE

God is both Lawgiver and Judge. His law is enshrined in the Ten Commandments — a series of Dos and Don'ts. Just as our lives are, but with this difference. God's Law is throughout a law of love, of his fatherly love for each one of us, his children. And that's why our Lord summed up the Dos and Don'ts of the Ten Commandments, like this.

You shall *love* the Lord your God with all your heart, and soul and mind.

This is the First Commandment. And the second is like it.

You shall *love* your neighbour as yourself.

On these two Commandments depend all the law and the prophets.

When we were children, our father and mother made rules for us, didn't they? Just as you make rules for your own children. If children are only obedient because they're afraid of being spanked, it's hurtful, isn't it? You make the rules for their own good, and you want them kept, out of love and respect for you.

God is our loving Father who wants us to keep the rules, not because we're afraid of him, but because we realise all he has done for us, and to love him for it. And to trust him to forgive us, no matter how low we've fallen.

All God has to say to the sorrowing sinner, is said in three words: "Sin no more." In the face of God's goodness, sin is mean, and if your heart's in the right place, sin will make you *feel* mean.

God's merciful love is so staggering, it doesn't leave us a leg to stand on, does it? So let us throw ourselves on our knees and at his mercy.

FACE TO FACE WITH LOVE

Our own secret sins are known only to ourselves and God. We're content to keep it that way, "delighting in the truth" about others. We're not so keen that others should know the truth about us.

All this is mere negative self-defence. But, as St. Paul explains, Christian charity is a positive, forward-looking, indestructible thing. "There is nothing love cannot face; there is no limit to its faith, its hope, and its endurance. Love will never come to an end."

It's been said that of all the arts whereby the mind of man, made in God's image, seeks to reflect God's beauty — poetry, painting, sculpture, music — it is music alone that will be carried over from time into eternity, because it is the most spiritual, the least materialistic of the arts.

Whether that is true or not, and we shall have music in Heaven, certainly Love will endure when Faith and Hope have lost their meaning and purpose. That's why St. Paul says that even here and now, of the three, Love is the greatest. Not love as the worldlings see it, a snatching of momentary pleasure which is cheap self-love, but an out-going giving, a forgetfulness of self in bowing to the betterment of another.

You can still, thank God, find that true unselfish love in this life, between husband and wife, parents and children, friend and friend, in the utter dedication of men and women, who see Christ in their fellow men and women.

We will find Love in all its purity, when we see each other as God sees us, and see him, not "as in a glass darkly, but face to face."

THE PROBLEM OF PAIN

The problem of pain puzzles everyone, believers and unbelievers alike, because suffering is a thing everyone has to face, sometime or other. It's part and parcel of our mortal life — the counterpart of pleasure which is also ours.

There are some people who meet the problem of pain with an air of indifference, chin held high, and a stiff upper lip — that we think so typically English. It isn't. It was the philosophy of the Stoics 300 years B.C. Others look on pain as the supreme evil. Avoid it at all costs if you can. But if you can't, then swamp it in an unending round of pleasures — eat, drink and be merry, for tomorrow we die.

Christ's answer to pain is the crucifix and, because it's a satisfying answer, there are some Catholics, often the best among us, who fall into the trap of glorifying suffering, almost idealising pain, rushing to meet it as an end in itself.

That is quite wrong. Pain as such is a curse and an evil. Yet it's inescapable. It won't be denied. It's a necessary evil. But you can make a virtue of necessity. And Christ showed us how.

It was in Gethsemane that for an hour his self-possession seemed to leave him, and he showed us how very much like us he was. For he, too, shuddered at the prospect of pain and prayed that he might escape it. Yet his all-too-human revulsion was quickly overcome by unshakeable resolution as he prayed: "Not my will but thine be done." The sweet obedience of Nazareth was carried through to the bitterness of Calvary, because it was the obedience of love. Pain suffered without love is purposeless.

ACCEPTANCE OF SUFFERING

Physical suffering in itself is an evil and therefore is, in itself, to be shunned. Indeed, Nature as God created it tells us what to do, by its instinctive shrinking from pain. Yet our physical make-up, having become what it is, imperfect through sin, cannot avoid suffering altogether, or even for long. The healthiest body is liable to injury by accident and, in the course of nature, to a wearing out, with discomforts attendant on loss of physical faculties.

For the maintenance of the life he has created, God provides the fruits of the earth that not only nourish the human body but heal it. And it is all part of God's plan that man's brain should work on his basic gifts to bring out their full powers, and make them available for the general well-being of mankind.

On our part, we have a duty not only to nourish but to cherish the bodily life God has given us. In other words, we are bound to use the means at our disposal to care for our health. This may entail the avoidance, or deadening, of pain by drugs. Yet there are physical aches and pains which don't impair our general health, and so we are under no obligation to alleviate them by chemical comforts, though we have every right to do so. And maybe we ought to seek such relief, at least in charity to others if, like the proverbial bear with the sore head, we get on their nerves.

If we can bear our minor ailments manfully, we should strive to do so, not merely as a means of self-discipline but as a small way of sharing Christ's cross and our minute reparation for our sins of self-indulgence and, indeed, of others too. The Christian without a cross doesn't exist. We all have our problems, personal or intimate, our own little heartaches, generally hidden away even from those around us.

COMFORT IN SUFFERING

None of us can eventually escape suffering, physical or mental, and it's generally both. That's an unavoidable part of our "human condition," as it's called. If that is so, if pain is part of God's plan for us, is it not therefore a good thing? Yes and No. Suffering, whether of mind or body, is in itself an evil thing. But it is something out of which good can be made.

Suffering should be easier for the Christian to accept. It was Christ's "instrument of salvation." It is Christ's call to his followers: "Take up your cross daily and follow me."

So there you are. The crosses of your daily life, however small, however great, are splinters of Christ's Cross which he asks you to carry with him. This means that your aches and pains, your worries and troubles, borne gladly for Christ's sake and with him, have a *redemptive* value. Christ, whose suffering was in itself sufficient to save us all from sin, nevertheless invites us all to share in his work of redemption by uniting our pain and sorrow with his.

So, what have you to complain about? It's a question I often ask myself. I've the usual aches of encroaching old age. And, far worse, the anxieties of one's own and other people's problems. And who can solve them? How can one help? I never cease to be ashamed of myself and proud of those of my own flock, grievously afflicted yet uncomplaining.

All of us have to suffer, but so often the greatest sufferers seem to have the grace to brush aside their own sorrows and cheer those who have come to comfort them.

HOPE OF LIFE AFTER DEATH

"I have immortal longings in me." When Shakespeare put these words in the mouth of Cleopatra, he was expressing a universal truth. (If there are exceptions, they prove the rule). We all cling instinctively to the hope of an after-life. With some of us, that hope is part and parcel of our faith, and we hold it with certainty.

Others would like it to be true. They echo — "I long to believe in immortality."

This longing for immortality, says Addison, is closely linked with fear of the opposite, of mortal life ending in oblivion:

> Whence this sacred dread, and inward horror,
> Of falling into nought? Why shrinks the soul
> Back on herself and startles at destruction?

The answer is that man yearns for survival because his soul is created in the image and likeness of the everlasting God.

> 'Tis the divinity that stirs within us;
> 'Tis heaven itself, that points out an hereafter,
> And intimates eternity to man.
> Eternity! thou pleasing, dreadful thought!

The thought of the hereafter must be both pleasant and full of dread because if, as we believe it, it exists, we shall live on there as we have lived here.

"The death of the good," wrote Belloc to a friend, "is their reward." Or, as St. Paul said of himself:

> I have fought the good fight: I have finished the race: I have redeemed my pledge: I look forward to the prize that is waiting for me, the prize I have earned. The Lord, the Judge whose award never goes amiss, will grant it to me when that day comes.

DEATH

As I write this I am alive; so are you as you read it, though by then I may no longer be. God alone knows when our time must come, but come it must. "There's nothing certain in man's life but this, that he must lose it."

But death, as we know it, the failure of some vital organ of the body, is not the end of the *person* we know. The spirit or soul survives the death of the body, the corruption of the flesh. The soul, we believe, is destined for unending life with its Creator. That is why in our Requiem Mass we say: "The sadness of death gives way to the bright promise of immortality. Lord, for your faithful people, life is changed, not ended."

We think of that new life as blessed by the vision of God forever. That is perfectly true. But is it also true that we who have loved in this life will renew our friendships in the next? That thought was put powerfully three hundred years ago by the Quaker, William Penn (founder of Pennsylvania), who wrote:

> They that love beyond the world cannot be separated by it. Death cannot kill what never dies: nor can spirits ever be divided that love and live in the same divine principle; the root and record of their friendship.
>
> Death is but crossing the worlds as friends do the seas; they live in one another still. But there must needs be present that love which is omnipresent. In that divine glass they see face to face; and their converse is free and pure. This is the comfort of friends; that though they may be said to die, yet their friendship and society are in the best sense, ever present, because immortal.

In the ups and downs of this life, most, maybe all of us, make and break friendships. But love that stands firm to the end will be taken up again forever in and with God. In Heaven we shall love one another for God's sake.

100

RE-LEARNING THE PAST

"No man can understand the present thoroughly without a knowledge of the past." Hilaire Belloc said that and the reason for it is simple. History, the story of man, is a living, continuously developing thing, like man himself. It isn't a series of static events unconnected and without influence on one another, as the school text books make it seem by pigeon-holing the past into "periods" locked fore and aft by dates.

One result of slanted history is that groups within a country, particularly religious groups, acquire a one-sided knowledge of their national past.

No English Catholics know enough about the Protestant martyrs to want to pay them honour. We're almost wholly ignorant of the men who died under Mary.

With our separated brethren the reverse is true. To either group the heroes of the other are a mere name, and a pretty bad name. Call them traitors or heretics, whichever school books you were brought up on.

Today Protestants do not hold present-day Catholics in any way responsible for these cruel deaths, just as Catholics today do not hold present-day Protestants in any way responsible for the execution of Catholics in the 16th and 17th centuries. Happily those days of intolerance are over and we all regret them. But regretting doesn't mean forgetting. On the contrary, it means remembering. It would be utterly unhistorical, indeed irrational, to say with a highly-respected prelate: "Let's forget the 16th century."

Far from militating against the ecumenical movement towards Christian Unity, knowing more about each other's past history and heroes can only help all of us to understand with sympathy situations, and the people caught up in them, which hitherto all of us have looked at with prejudice and bigotry, because that's the way we were taught. We all need re-teaching, and should do it ourselves by re-reading.

REUNION ON ITS WAY

The reunion of Christians is the object of a volume of prayer added to year by year and clearly receiving an answer in the gathering momentum of interest in the reunion of Christendom among our separated brethren.

When Canterbury and Rome met, there was immediate and cordial response from the Holy Father, but the original initiative came from Dr. Fisher and we should remember with humility his remark that accompanied their handshake: "We are making history."

The rest of us, Catholic and Protestant, must swim understandingly with the tide of history. There is still a long way to go. In the Churchillian phrase, the end isn't yet in sight, we're not even at the beginning of the end, but, please God, we're at the end of the beginning.

"We have given a good example," said the Archbishop, "and good examples are often imitated by others." Pope John's comment at the time was: "One must place trust in God without hastening judgments and forecasts. The Lord works on souls."

This sentiment was echoed in Rome itself by Dr. Fisher, who asked his fellow-Protestants to join him in praying "that the Holy Spirit may so release us as to do his work through and in and for the Church."

Humble gratitude to God for graces, given to us through no merit of our own, must be coupled with recognition of the fact that God gives grace to Protestants too, above all through the sacramental brotherhood of Baptism which makes our separated brethren our brothers in Christ.

They often respond to grace better than we do — and are more sincere and single-minded than we. All this makes them worthy of admiration and respect and will spur us on to pray with greater fervour and humility that we all may be one.

UNITY IN CHRIST

"Our Unity in Christ, our Disunity as Churches" was a main subject of discussion among 160 Christian denominations that met in 1954 under the auspices of the World Council of Churches.

In the 16th century, abuses within the Church of Christ aroused an outcry against those who had inherited authority conferred by our Lord on his Apostles. All this has led progressively in the last 400 years to a multiplication of man-made sects originating from man-made differences of opinion. The prophet's words have been fulfilled: "They have sown the wind and they reap the whirlwind."

To their great credit, the denominations have, in the last half-century, not only deplored their differences but are seeking to remove them. Their dilemma is that they seek sincerely for unity, while rejecting the authority that alone can guide them into unity. All agree, as we do, that "on the basis of the New Testament the Church of Christ is one." Yet the World Council, in which they meet as churches, "disavows any thought of becoming a single unified Church structure dominated by a centralised administrative authority."

And yet what alternative is there to one Church, teaching one doctrine with Christ's divine commission and authority? It can only be an ever-growing number of self-authorised teachers, each differing, however slightly, from the other.

That explains the admiration often voiced for the Catholic Church by many who do not as yet give her their allegiance. And therefore her affectionate and prayerful care extends to all those who are now seeking, in ways however diverse, to restore that unity, so that once more there may be but "One Fold and One Shepherd."

FACING LIFE WITH COURAGE

If you've been hard hit by life, materially or mentally, physically or spiritually, you're doing no good to anybody, least of all yourself, by taking it out on God. If you do, you're still left with your burden, but alone, without the One who can, and will eventually, explain it and here and now will help you to bear it.

Accept our Lord's open invitation: "Come to Me, all you that labour and are burdened and you shall find rest for your souls."

Here's a tale for you and every word is true:

A man I know was badly injured by a drunken motorist at the age of 15. His leg was amputated, but he married happily, until, after six years, his wife left him for another man. Yet he was determined to make the best of life and work for others, which he did. Then he got the idea of starting up a pen friendship with a cripple worse off than himself.

He was put in touch with a fellow who had been struck on the head by a cricket ball at the age of nine and who had lost all use of his arms and legs; an incurable who had been in hospital for over 40 years. This man answered my friend with a three-page letter from which cheerfulness, optimism and good spirits shone through every sentence. And how do you think he ended his letter? "I thank God," he said, "I thank God that I'm able to write my own letters by holding the pen in my mouth."

Such a glorious example of courage and trust and faith makes us feel very humble, doesn't it? Almost as if we hadn't even begun to understand Christ, and him crucified.

BY OUR FRUITS

Behaviourism is nowadays a favourite pastime, at least in America, where to be "psyched" forms part and parcel of one's periodic medical check-up, so I'm told.

It was Francis Bacon who wrote: "Men discover themselves at unawares." By this he meant that, constantly and without realising it, we reveal character and temperament through such physical characteristics as the way we walk, the poise of head and shoulders, the set of chin and jaw, the look in the eyes. All of these are affected and influenced by our mental development over the years (who was it said that a person is responsible for his or her face by the age of forty?), until we settle into one or other of various types.

The study of handwriting is well-known as a means of judging character. But the human voice is the most revealing index of personality, not just the inflection or intonation, the loudness or softness of the voice, but its ground-tone quality.

It tells of determination or weakness of will, of industry and effort, of tenacity and irresolution. It speaks, straight to the ear, of intellectual power, of concentration of thought, of rapidity or slowness of mind, of alertness or dullness of perception, of feeling and emotion; of justice, sincerity, straightness, honour.

The point about all this is that we, body-soul creatures, reveal our spiritual qualities to one another through our physical characteristics, for as the philosophers say, "there is nothing in the mind that isn't first in the senses." However much we may at times try to conceal our real selves, we can never wholly succeed for, as an acute observer once remarked: "Nature is often hidden; sometimes overcome; seldom extinguished."

COPING WITH STRESS

What about "Stress" or, rather, how to cope with it? Ask yourself, what's the cause of it? The direct approach to the person or problem is probably the best. And remember, not every argument is worth trying to win. Only when there's a principle involved. And don't be weighed down by your failures. Think of your successes. It will do you good. And seek advice. Confiding in a friend can uncoil the tightly wound spring of tension. And do something for others. "Reaching out" can take the focus off self and reduce stress caused by brooding.

Do one thing at a time. You'll get more done with less hustle, and danger of heart attacks, if you concentrate on one thing at a time. Put on the brake and take a break. Do something else. Go for a walk. Physical exercise can refresh you after heavy mental strain; and a book or TV can relax you after demanding physical work. So can meditation and prayer.

A favourite saying of my mother was: "Don't worry; it may never happen." Some people are natural worriers. I heard of one woman who suddenly realised that fears were ruining her peace of mind. So she took a pencil and made a list of her worries. Here is her conclusion:

40% will never happen.
30% past decisions one can't alter.
12% criticism by others, most of it untrue.
10% about one's health, which gets worse with worry!
 8% genuine cause for worry about one's real problems.

So the lady in question added it up and found that 92% of her worries had no foundation in fact.

Why not try this exercise yourself and see what your worry balance sheet looks like?

THE NEED FOR RELAXATION

Relaxation. Recreation. What do the words mean? To relax is to make one less tense, to relieve one from nervous strain and tension. And, goodness knows, most of us suffer from that nowadays. Things and people "get on our nerves." We're tensed up. The tension snaps and we say and do things that we don't mean. We become irritable and snappy with our colleagues at work. And even more often with those at home — we've lost control. We need to relax, to restore our spirit and our strength. But that's easier said than done.

You hear people talk of life nowadays as a rat-race. I didn't expect to find that in the dictionary, but there it was described as "a violent, senseless, competitive activity or rush." Would you agree?

If you commute to and from work you'd admit that, day in and day out, you're caught up in a violent competitive activity or rush. Is it all so senseless? You'll probably say you have to keep up the pace, otherwise you'll fall behind in the rat-race — and in the standard of living you've set yourself. That will happen in any case and far more disastrously, if physical exhaustion and nervous tension land you with a coronary — nature's answer to the overworked.

I had a mild one years ago, and was told by my doctor it was a hint from the Almighty to put on the brakes, to slow down.

The point is, it's senseless to kill yourself to live. You must, whatever your job, however rewarding it is, give yourself time to relax, and to re-create, to refresh, to rebuild both your body and your spirit.

FACING UP TO LIFE

"If only I could get away from it all!" The desire to "run away" is deeply rooted in all of us — so many of us try it. But as long as we're on this spinning globe, our work is this: to accept responsibility and bring some divine love into our very earthy difficulties.

"Nobody cares about me." Like most half-truths, this statement can be an excuse for doing less than we should. Once you stop allowing resentment to distort your life, you can put past experience to work for others. You may even help them to avoid the same mistakes you have made. "Bear one another's burdens, and so fulfil the law of Christ" (Galatians 6: 2).

"I just can't keep up with everything." When personal problems appear unmanageable, world events totally beyond comprehension, we should resist the temptation to pull back into a private world, or even a fantasy world. Discover the real world. Revitalise your thinking. Develop your unused powers. Find new meaning in purposeful service to others.

"What's the use of trying?" To try when there is little hope is to risk failure. Not to try at all is to guarantee it. "You can't beat the system." Anger or dissatisfaction with any "system" will never change it. Doing something will. Once our excuses are set aside, we can move ahead with the confidence that even a small candle of constructive, purposeful action is, in its own way, greater than all the darkness.

Most of the time, people will be as positive or negative as we expect them to be. God puts an astonishing amount of trust in each one of us.

ACCEPTING OURSELVES AS WE ARE

"I just can't take it any more." Do you honestly think you would exchange your troubles for those of somebody else? Centuries ago, Socrates concluded that, all things considered, you'd probably settle for your own. "If all our misfortunes were laid in one pile from which everyone had to take an equal portion," he said, "most people would be content to take back their own and depart."

Learn to live with the problems you can't change, and ask God for the strength to do something about the ones you can.

Realism is the first step in the conquest of self-pity. "My life is so empty." People who complain about the emptiness of their lives fail to realise that redoubled efforts to understand others are often more effective than "picking over the raw bones of their own psyche." Signs of emotional immaturity can in many cases, lead to habitual self-pity.

"Nothing I do makes a bit of difference." The world is full of human want. We must take our eyes off ourselves to see it. We don't have to look far to find someone for whom our actions can make a great difference. "I haven't got what it takes." A man who lost his sight and both hands in an accident now serves as rehabilitation counsellor for the mentally ill. No matter what our limitations, each of us can do something with God's help, to ease the burden of other people. By doing so we perform a valuable service and add meaning to our own lives.

The person who finds satisfaction in living for others may grow old but remains youthful in outlook. "Gladly, therefore, I will glory in my infirmities, that the strength of Christ may dwell in me" (Cor., 12: 10).

THE NEED FOR DISCIPLINE

The late Lord Mountbatten once spoke wise words about discipline. He said that discipline isn't a question of touching your cap but a recognition of ability. He gave as an example the stockbroker who takes orders from his gardener on how to plant bulbs. He then went on to say, what we all know only too well nowadays, that "discipline," in general, is anathema to youth. It has become a dirty word.

He explained what we Catholics of all people should know, that discipline comes from the Latin and it means teaching, the instruction of disciples, and he added:

> I am not trying to be pompous but being disciplined is being able to control yourself to your best advantage. Why is the new generation kicking over the traces? Because there has been a lack of discipline, a lack of teaching by their parents, and yet youth lacks belief in its parents. Young people should give their parents credit for what they have done.

But should they? Lord Mountbatten raised many questions that demand an answer. A main cause for the rot that has set in is surely the steady decline of sanctions, religious, moral and legal, against discipline. Crime is punished far less severely than it was. Immorality goes scot-free simply because society has no moral standards.

Morality has become a meaningless word, replaced by "I do as I please because I recognise no one more important than myself to please; and I do what I do for 'kicks'." That's the current fashionable yardstick of behaviour. In a TV programme a self-confessed shoplifter said she didn't think of what she did as stealing. She just did it for "kicks."

Short of kicking back, which the law of the land is so timid about, the best we can do is to show by word and example that the law of God is there still to be respected and obeyed in the Ten Commandments. This brings us back to discipline and discipleship, which our Divine Lord put very simply, "Learn of me . . . Follow me."

GOD IS ALWAYS WITH US

I'm sure you've heard this quotation, though you may not know who wrote it: "One is nearer to God's Heart in a garden than anywhere else on earth." Do you agree? I hope not, because it isn't true! You're nearest to God in your own soul, made in the image and likeness of God himself. But no matter where you are you're close to God, in fact you can't get away from him, because the Creator is everywhere by his sustaining power, as the Psalmist says:

> Where can I go then to take refuge from thy spirit, to hide from thy view? If I should climb up to heaven thou art there; if I sink down to the world beneath, thou art present still. If I would wing my way eastwards or find a dwelling beyond the western sea, still I would find thee beckoning to me, thy right hand upholding me.

So God is with us at all times, and everywhere, even within the four walls of a lonely room. Yet, because, as we say, God made the country and man made the town, we do seem extra close to God amid the glories of Nature that mirror the beauty of the Almighty Mind that fashioned it. It was our Lord's love of Nature that made the poet see in it a certain sacramental character — an outward sign of the grace that is Christ:

> *I see his blood upon the rose*
> *And in the stars the glory of his eyes.*
> *His body gleams amid eternal snows.*
> *His tears fall from the skies.*
> *I see his face in every flower.*
> *The thunder and the singing of the birds*
> *Are but his voice and carven by his power*
> *Rocks are his unwritten words.*
> *All pathways by his feet are worn;*
> *His strong heart stirs the ever-beating sea.*
> *His crown of thorns is twined with every thorn,*
> *His cross is every tree.*

THE VALUE OF TIME

The phrase "Earning one's living" is a fine one, full of meaning. As each one of us has a right to life, so each of us has a right to a living wage. It's a right for which in the past some workers have had to fight.

But it's so easy to forget that a right brings with it a responsibility. When it's a question of work, that means all without exception are responsible in conscience for giving of one's best and fullest both in time and in skill. Any honest job honestly done is God's will for us. You can't divorce your duty to man from your duty to God. So conscientiousness in doing a full job is due not only to the employer who pays you. It's due also (and especially in these critical days) to the community, to the nation and to God.

So "Produce! produce! Were it but the pitifullest, infinitesimal fraction of a product, produce it in God's name! 'Tis the utmost thou hast in thee." (That's Carlyle.)

Now, earning your living means earning the right to leisure and relaxation. Maybe your employer has no say in what you do with your "free time," but God has. All time is God's time, lent to you for use and not abuse. You are still responsible to God for the sensible and full use of leisure and rest from work.

Time wasted has a way of wreaking its own revenge. "An idle mind is the Devil's workshop." That's a trite saying but it's very true. In the matter of time wasted and lost, there's no second chance. It's gone forever. "Time goes, we say. Ah no! Alas Time stays — we go." So don't talk of "killing time." — You can't do it anyway. Time kills you.

112

FREEDOM OF SPEECH

Speech, the faculty to express thought, is God's greatest gift to man. That gift is largely thwarted unless men are allowed to speak freely and openly to expound their ideas. And yet because ideas expressed persuasively are the most forceful way of influencing others, it is lawful for the society in which a man lives to restrict freedom of speech, otherwise the well-being of the general community is in danger of being undermined.

To propagate treason, especially when a country is at war, is rightly considered a crime, punishable at least by silencing the speaker. There was a time in the history of Christian Europe when both Church and State shared the grim task of stamping out false ideas in faith and morals.

One has only to read of the anarchical teaching of the Catharists in 13th century southern France, with their belief in the virtues of starvation, suicide and abortion, their sanction of free love and unnatural vice, to understand, if not to approve, the ruthlessness of the Inquisition founded to cope with the evil.

In the 16th century the silencing (by physical persecution) of religious doctrines considered false and subversive was regarded as normal by all our Tudor sovereigns, while in Germany Lutherans killed off Anabaptists and in Geneva, Calvin was merciless to anyone, even his best friend, who questioned his theocratic rule.

Nowadays, no one would dream of adopting such inhuman practices, yet the pendulum has swung to the other extreme, even in the Catholic Church. The new found freedom of speech that has emerged since the Second Vatican Council is laudable in principle. In practice, it is often deplorable.

This change in the attitude of authority by no means relieves the rank-and-file Catholic of that duty of vigilance which our Lord impressed on his followers: "Beware of false prophets," he cried at the end of his Sermon on the Mount.

THE MEDIA

You could describe civilisation as the development of man's mind from semi-savage to cultured intellect. And this has been brought about by the communication of ideas. For long centuries it took place slowly through the spoken and the written word; but, also for long centuries, the impact of mind upon mind, though all were and are creatures in God's image, was only on the few. In other words, although all men have the potential of literacy, only a minority have achieved it, even today.

The break-through came with Gutenberg's invention of moving type in 1440. This made available to millions what had hitherto been read only by a few thousands, the heritage of pagan and Christian literature. But it still took a long time to make men literate, and it hasn't been fully achieved even today.

Another breakthrough, greater even than that of Gutenberg's, has been that of Radio and Television. Here we have means of communication of facts and ideas, reaching the masses in ways often easier and more attractive than through the printed word, whether in books or the popular press.

Books? I remember a remark of Hilaire Belloc, many years ago, that people don't read books, they refer to them. He said that at a time when "Penguins" were becoming popular, and it is still true, even in our age of paper-backs.

A recent report on education said that adults are allergic to reading; the type of person once referred to as "the general public" now spends more time on the spoken than on the written word. The latter requires more mental concentration than the former, and most of us are so mentally lazy that we take the line of least resistance. We turn a switch on and listen. Even between Radio and Television we tend to make the easier choice, which means more look and less listen.

DRIVE WITH CARE

Be alive to others on the road is the slogan to impress upon all the personal responsibility of each of us for road safety. The casualty figures are horrifying; a death every 76 minutes, an injury every 93 seconds.

Have you ever thought of what injury, short of death, can do? Here is the result of one, reported in the press: "Local man, aged 36, dies after 15 years in hospital, following car accident, in which he was totally disabled."

Think of all that lies behind that laconic announcement. Fifteen years of staring at the same ceiling; 180 months of complete helplessness; 780 weeks of utter hopelessness; 5,475 days of waiting for the night; 5,475 nights longing for the dawn; 131,400 hours imprisoned amid four walls; fading flowers, medical smells, frustrated sympathy; 7,884,000 minutes merely hanging on to life, without hope, the spirit shrinking in stagnation; 473,040,000 seconds awaiting death at 36 after 15 years of dying.

A tragedy as terrifying as that can arise from some little fault or careless inattention, such as we all commit pretty well every day of our driving life and get away with. Maybe one day we won't, unless the full measure of our responsibility as driver, passenger or pedestrian weighs prayerfully upon our minds and hearts every moment we're using the roads.

Author of Life, never let me bring death to those for whom thou gavest thy life. Help me to drive with steady hand, sure eye and full control and protect from every mishap all who accompany me.

115

COURAGE OF CONVICTIONS

"Courage," wrote G. K. Chesterton, "is almost a contradiction in terms. It means a strong desire to live taking the form of a readiness to die."

We're all fascinated by deeds of great physical courage, confronting death or danger. Yet such bravery is often an instinctive reaction. It is moral, rather than physical, courage that deserves our praise.

Our mind is able to distinguish good from evil. Our will, which controls — or fails to control — our actions, has therefore a moral responsibility to do what the mind tells us is right and to avoid what the mind tells us is wrong. To act up to that, in face of danger of difficulty or the pressure of public opinion, is Moral Courage.

All of us, at some time or other, are called upon to show the courage of our convictions. When the Faith comes under fire of criticism or a sneer, we ought to reveal ourselves as Catholics and defend the Faith. When we hear scandalous slander or calumny of others, we should be prepared to show disapproval.

On occasion, the easy way out is to stay silent. No one may know what you ought to have done, except you and God. It is he who calls upon you, through the voice of conscience, to be morally courageous and speak out.

Most difficult of all is when, as a person in authority, you are faced with a decision, either to let things go on as they always have done or to make changes that you are convinced are for the better, but which make you thoroughly unpopular, even with your friends. In all such situations, "Trust God and do the right."

BONUS YEARS

We're all growing older, living longer, yet retiring earlier than the Psalmist's span of three score and ten. How are we going to use our "bonus" years?

The deep-seated yearning by people of every age to be purposeful is rooted in the creative activity of God himself. Many older persons echo the words of the Psalmist: "They shall still increase in a fruitful old age" (Psalm 92: 15).

What are the advantages of retirement? One man put it well when he said: "Retirement is a time for a rebirth." It is important for people to retire *to* not just *from* something. Retirement can be a time to do some well-deserved relaxing; an opportunity to seek emotional tranquillity and engage in constructive leisure; a release from the burdens of responsibility.

Loneliness afflicts many. ("No one has knocked on my door for months.") Inability to clean and repair, to shop or cook, to get doctors or keep up with friends are common complaints. Inactivity saps vigour of mind and body. Malnutrition appears to be a major cause of mental ills among the elderly. Treat yourself with respect. This means proper personal care, diet, dressing up on occasions — and not apologising for your age.

Offer advice only when asked. Be patient with those who give it to you unbidden — present company included! Keep in touch with your friends. Make reasonable efforts, too, at meeting new ones. Maintain whatever independence you can. But don't let sensitivity keep you from seeking needed aid. Accept your limitations gracefully.

Develop your spiritual life. Read at least a few verses of the Bible daily and reflect on them. Keep your prayer uncomplicated but try to raise your thoughts frequently to God. Think it over.